UNIT 4

SEX EDUCATION ACTIVITIES

UNIT 4

SEX EDUCATION ACTIVITIES

PATRICIA RIZZO TONER

Just for the HEALTH of It!
Health Curriculum Activities Library

**THE CENTER FOR APPLIED
RESEARCH IN EDUCATION**
West Nyack, New York 10995

© 1993 by

THE CENTER FOR APPLIED
RESEARCH IN EDUCATION
West Nyack, New York

10   9   8   7   6   5   4   3   2

Library of Congress Cataloging-in-Publication Data
Toner, Patricia Rizzo
    Sex education activities / Patricia Rizzo Toner.
      p.   cm. — (Just for the health of it! ; unit 4)
    ISBN 0-87628-851-4
    1. Sex instruction for teenagers.   I. Center for Applied Research
in Education.   II. Title.   III. Series.
HQ35.T65   1993
613.9'07—dc20   93-14860
                                                              CIP

ISBN   0-87628-851-4

**The Center for Applied Research
in Education,** Professional Publishing
West Nyack, New York 10995
Simon & Schuster, A Paramount Communications Company

Printed in the United States of America

DEDICATION

To Section 9-3 Health at Holland Junior High,
Council Rock School District, 1991-1992:

Carla, Jeff, Tim, Melinda, Crystal, Ilana, Andy, Jason,
EJ, Alisha, Lynn, Rachael, Meredith, Cheryl, Melissa,
Nicole, Dorie, Jida, Chris, Denise, Elana, Mike, Dante,
Brian, Tim, Susie, Rob, Shawna

Thanks for a year I will never forget. Need I say more?
May you find all the happiness life has to offer.

Patricia Rizzo Toner

ABOUT THE AUTHOR

Patricia Rizzo Toner, M.Ed., has taught Health and Physical Education in the Council Rock School District, Holland, Pennsylvania, for over 19 years and she has also coached gymnastics and field hockey. She is the co-author of three books: *What Are We Doing in Gym Today?*, *You'll Never Guess What We Did in Gym Today!*, and *How to Survive Teaching Health*. Besides her work as a teacher, Pat is also a freelance cartoonist, and a member of the American Alliance of Health, Physical Education, Recreation and Dance. She received the Hammond Service Award, the Marianna G. Packer Book Award and was named to *Who's Who in American Education*.

ABOUT <u>JUST FOR THE HEALTH OF IT!</u>

Just for the Health of It! was developed to give you, the health teacher, new ways to present difficult-to-teach subjects and to spark your students' interest in day-to-day health classes. It includes over 540 ready-to-use activities organized for your teaching convenience into six separate, self-contained units focusing on six major areas of health education.

Each unit provides ninety classroom-tested activities printed in a full-page format and ready to be photocopied as many times as needed for student use. Many of the activities are illustrated with cartoon figures to enliven the material and help inject a touch of humor into the health curriculum.

The following briefly describes each of the six units in the series:

Unit 1: *Consumer Health and Safety Activities* helps students recognize advertising techniques, compare various products and claims, understand consumer rights, distinguish between safe and dangerous items, become familiar with safety rules, and more.

Unit 2: *Diet and Nutrition Activities* focuses on basic concepts and skills such as the four food groups, caloric balance or imbalance, the safety of diets, food additives, and vitamin deficiency diseases.

Unit 3: *Relationships and Communication Activities* explores topics such as family relationships, sibling rivalry, how to make friends, split-level communications, assertiveness and aggressiveness, dating, divorce, and popularity.

Unit 4: *Sex Education Activities* teaches about the male and female reproductive systems, various methods of contraception ranging from abstinence to mechanical and chemical methods, sexually transmitted diseases, the immune system, pregnancy, fetal development, childbirth, and more.

Unit 5: *Stress Management and Self-Esteem Activities* examines the causes and signs of stress and teaches ways of coping with it. Along with these, the unit focuses on various elements of building self-esteem such as appearance, values, self-concept, success and confidence, personality, and character traits.

Unit 6: *Substance Abuse Prevention Activities* deals with the use and abuse of tobacco, alcohol, and other drugs and examines habits ranging from occasional use to addiction. It also promotes alternatives to drug use by examining peer pressure situations, decision-making, and where to seek help.

To help you mix and match activities from the series with ease, all of the activities in each unit are designated with two letters to represent each resource as follows: Sex Education (SE), Substance Abuse Prevention (SA), Relationships and Communication (RC), Stress Management and Self-Esteem (SM), Diet and Nutrition (DN), and Consumer Health and Safety (CH).

About Unit 4

Sex Education Activities, Unit 4 in *Just for the Health of It!*, gives you ninety ready-to-use activities for teaching one of the most difficult subjects in an organized, comfortable manner. The activities include reproducibles to hand out to students, innovative games, puzzles, and other techniques to enhance your presentations.

You can use these aids in any way you wish—to introduce a particular subject, to heighten student interest at a given point in a lesson, or to reinforce what students have already learned. Complete answer keys for the activity sheets are provided at the end of the unit. You may keep these for your own use or place a copy at some central location for student self-checking.

For quick selection of appropriate activities, the table of contents provides general and specific topic heads and a complete listing of all worksheets and other activities in the unit. The ninety activities are organized into seven main sections, including:

Puberty. This section helps students learn about changes that take place in the male and female body during puberty. The main topics include:
- Understanding Bodily Changes
- Hormones

Reproductive Systems. More than ten activities in this section help students understand reproduction by focusing on these and other topics:
- The Female Reproductive System
- The Male Reproductive System
- Diseases and Disorders

Pregnancy and Childbirth. Pregnancy and development of the embryo and fetus are covered in this section under two main topics:
- Signs and Stages of Pregnancy
- Pregnancy and Childbirth

Contraception. This section offers more than fifteen activities that focus on contraception. Some of the main topics are:
- Chemical Methods of Contraception
- Mechanical Methods of Contraception
- Abstinence Methods of Contraception

Sexually Transmitted Diseases. The twenty activities in this section cover one dozen sexually transmitted diseases under two main topics:
- STD Signs, Symptoms, and Solutions
- AIDS

Sexual Decision Making and Topics for Discussion. This section provides fifteen activities to promote student decision making with topics such as:
- Teen Pregnancy Options
- Consequences of Intercourse Before Marriage
- Practicing Refusal Skills

General Review Activities. The final section features additional supplementary activities such as a bingo game to review sex education vocabulary and a question-and-answer game.

All of the reproducibles and activities in this unit are numbered consecutively and keyed to the unit with the letters SE, representing the Sex Education component of the series. These worksheets, games, and activities can be put directly into your lessons.

Motivating students isn't always easy, but I hope this resource will make a "difficult" subject one you'll love to teach.

Patricia Rizzo Toner

CONTENTS

PUBERTY

- **Understanding Bodily Changes**

- **Hormones**

ACTIVITY 1: GROW UP!
(Understanding puberty)

Concept/
Description: Many physical changes occur during adolescence.

Objective: On the accompanying worksheets, students will correctly fill in the physical changes that males and females experience during puberty.

Materials: Understanding puberty worksheets (see SE-1, SE-2)
Pens or pencils

Directions: 1. Ask students to tell you the physical changes that they think a girl or boy might experience between the ages of 11 and 18 years. If correct, have them place the answers on the Understanding puberty worksheets.
2. When completed, explain that these changes happen to everyone and that it is perfectly normal for the changes to occur at different times in different individuals.
3. Ask if the students think this varying rate of change could cause embarrassment and if so, how? Ask for ideas for coping with the changes or accompanying embarrassment.

2

Name _____ **Date** _____

PUBERTY IN FEMALES (SE-1)

Understanding puberty worksheet

PUBERTY IN MALES (SE-2)

Understanding puberty worksheet

ENDOCRINE FUNCTIONS (SE-3)

DIRECTIONS: Label the parts of the Endocrine System and match each gland to its function by placing the correct letter in the blank.

_____ 1. thyroid gland

_____ 2. pineal gland

_____ 3. adrenal glands

_____ 4. pituitary gland

_____ 5. pancreas

_____ 6. ovaries

_____ 7. testes

_____ 8. parathyroids

_____ 9. thymus gland

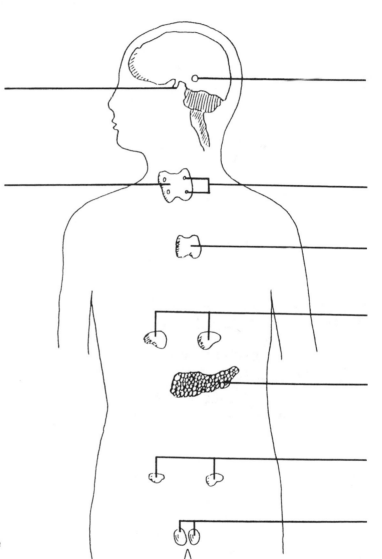

a. secretes a digestive juice and produces insulin
b. located near the heart and may play an important role in the immune system
c. produces thyroxine
d. master gland that has many regulatory functions
e. four small glands that regulate calcium and phosphorus
f. located in the brain and may have to do with sexual development
g. produces testosterone and sperm cells
h. located at the top of each kidney and secretes steroid hormones
i. produces egg cells, estrogen, and progesterone

Name _____ **Date** _____

UNDERSTANDING HORMONES (SE-4)

DIRECTIONS: Next to each endocrine gland listed is a list of the hormones that the gland secretes. Find what job or function each hormone performs and describe what occurs when the gland is overactive or underactive.

GLAND	HORMONE	FUNCTION	OVER	UNDER
pituitary	somatropic			
	TSH			
	ACTH			
	FSH			
	LH			
	antidiuretic			
	oxytocin			
thyroid	thyroxine			
adrenals	steroids			
	aldosterone			
	cortisone			
	adrenaline			
pancreas	glucagon			
	insulin			
ovaries	estrogen			
	progesterone			
testes	testosterone			

© 1993 by The Center for Applied Research in Education

ENDOCRINE MATCH-UP (SE-5)

DIRECTIONS: Match the endocrine gland with the letter of the hormone or condition associated with it. There may be more than one letter for each gland.

GLAND

_____ 1. pituitary

_____ 2. thyroid

_____ 3. adrenals

_____ 4. pancreas

_____ 5. ovaries

_____ 6. testes

HORMONE/FUNCTION/DISORDER

a. progesterone

b. somatotropic hormone

c. adrenaline

d. cortisone

e. sperm cells

f. FSH

g. egg cells

h. insulin

i. dwarfism

j. estrogen

k. acromegaly

l. thyroxine

m. steroids

n. testosterone

o. TSH

p. goiter

REPRODUCTIVE SYSTEMS

- **The Female Reproductive System**

- **The Male Reproductive System**

- **Comprehension Check**

- **Diseases and Disorders**

FEMALE REPRODUCTIVE SYSTEM DIAGRAM (SE-6)

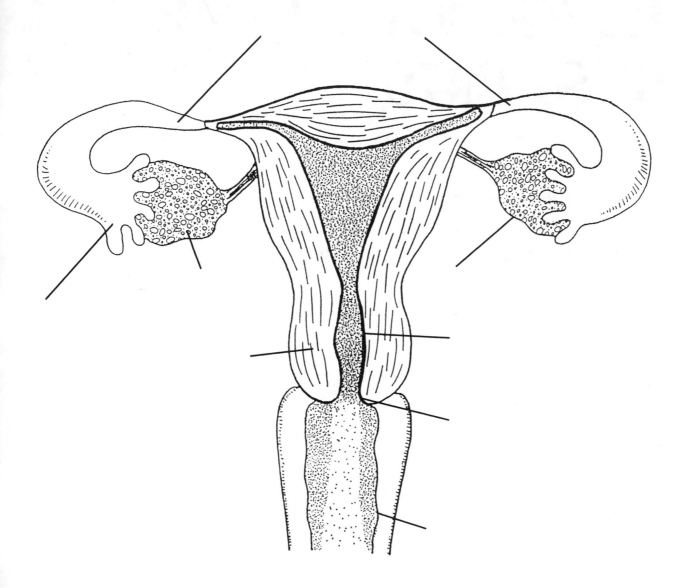

DIRECTIONS: Using the words below, label the parts of the female reproductive system:

CERVIX	UTERUS	OVUM	FALLOPIAN TUBE
FIMBRIA	OVARY	VAGINA	UTERINE LINING

FEMALE REPRODUCTIVE SYSTEM (SE-7)
External View

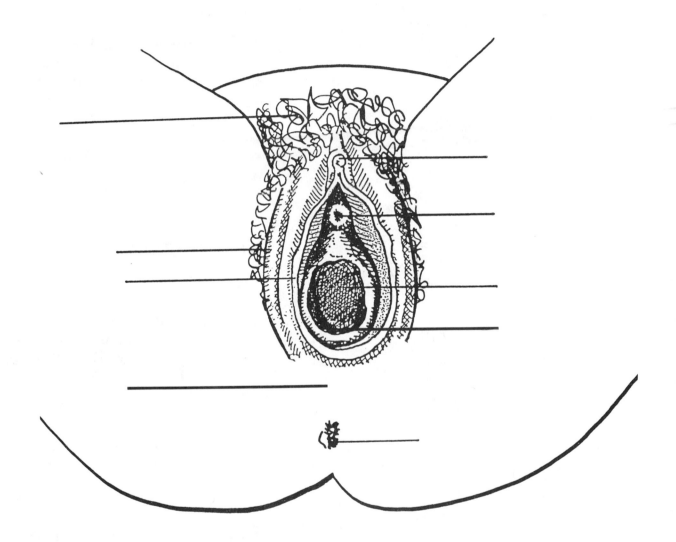

DIRECTIONS: Label the diagram using the words below:

PUBIC HAIR	CLITORIS	VAGINA
INNER LABIA	OUTER LABIA	ANUS
URETHRA	HYMEN	PERINEUM

THE MENSTRUAL CYCLE (SE-8)

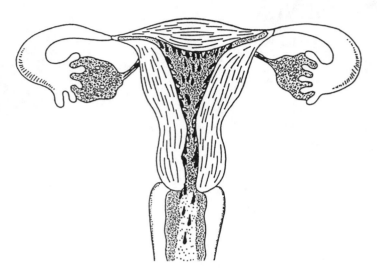

DURING MENSTRUATION

Days 1-5:

Menstruation occurs and the lining of the uterus, with a small amount of blood, leaves the body. At this time another egg is maturing in the ovary.

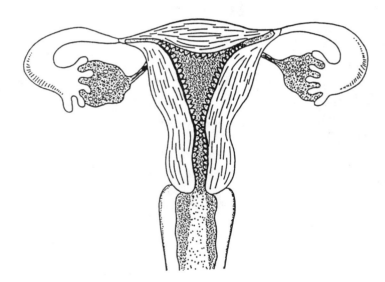

AFTER MENSTRUATION:

Days 6-15:

The lining of the uterus repairs itself and once again prepares for a fertilized egg. Around days 13 to 15 an egg is released from an ovary. This is called OVULATION.

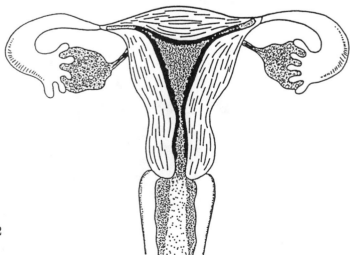

BEFORE MENSTRUATION:

Days 16-28:

If the egg is fertilized by the male sperm cell, it embeds itself in the wall of the uterus. If the egg is not fertilized, the blood vessels in the wall of the uterus shrink and break down. Then menstruation begins again.

Name _____ **Date** _____

THE FEMALE REPRODUCTIVE SYSTEM (SE-9)

DIRECTIONS: Using the sixteen words provided, fill in the blanks to make this explanation of the female reproductive system correct. Each word will be used only once.

cervix

clitoris

egg cells

estrogen

Fallopian tubes

hymen

labia

menstruation

ovaries

ovulation

ovum

progesterone

puberty

sperm cell

uterus

vagina

First, _____ _____ are produced in two almond-shaped organs known

as the _____. During the process of _____, a

mature egg (_____) is released and enters one of two _____

_____. For a few days the egg cell travels towards the pear-shaped

_____. The lining of this organ thickens in preparation for a fertil-

ized egg. If the egg is not fertilized by the male _____ _____, it will

leave the body together with the lining of the uterus and a small amount of blood.   This is

called _____.

The lower portion of the uterus is called the _____ and is a

common site of cancer in women.   The female organ of intercourse is the

_____. A circular fold of skin is usually present at the entrance to

this organ and is called the _____. Outside of this organ are folds of

skin covered with pubic hair known as the _____. Between these

skin folds is a small, round, sensitive area of skin called the _____.

The development of the reproductive system is triggered by the hormones

_____ and _____, which cause many physical

changes in a girl.   This period of change is called _____.

MALE REPRODUCTIVE SYSTEM DIAGRAM (SE-10)

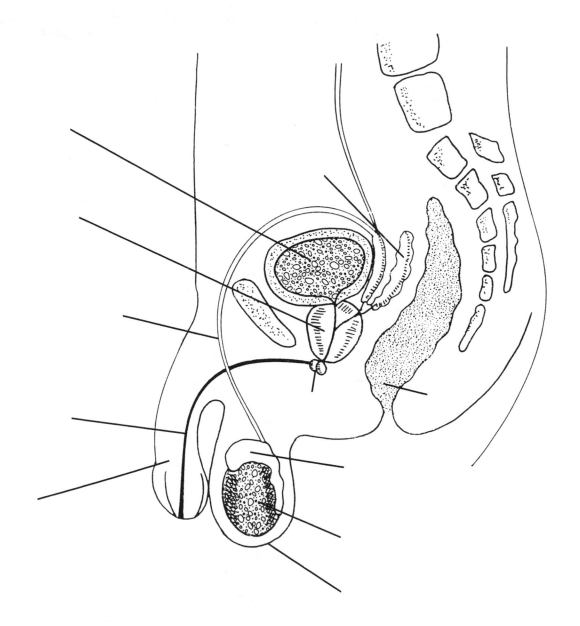

DIRECTIONS: Using the words below, label the parts of the male reproductive system:

PENIS	RECTUM	BLADDER	TESTICLE
URETHRA	EPIDIDYMIS	PROSTATE	COWPER'S GLAND
SCROTUM	VAS DEFERENS	SEMINAL VESICLE	

THE MALE REPRODUCTIVE SYSTEM (SE-11)

DIRECTIONS: Using the fifteen words provided, fill in the blanks to make this explanation of the male reproductive system correct. Each will be used only once.

Cowper's gland
epididymis
erection
nocturnal emissions
orgasm
penis
prostate
scrotum

semen
seminal vesicle
sperm
testes
urine
urethra
vas deferens

First, _____ are produced in the small seminiferous tubules of the _____. These oval-shaped glands are protected by a sac called the _____. After the sperm cells are produced, they are stored in a large coiled tube on the outer surface of each testicle called the _____. From this tube the sperm go into a larger tube called the _____ _____, which eventually carries them to the external male reproductive organ, the _____. Along the way sperm is nourished by a sugary fluid from the _____ _____, a chemical fluid from the _____ which is the most common site of cancer in men, and fluid from the _____ _____ which are two small glands located near the bladder. These fluids plus the sperm cells combine to form _____, the fluid ejaculated from the penis during _____. Before a male can ejaculate, the spongy tissue surrounding the penis becomes engorged with blood causing the penis to become stiff and hard. This is known as an _____. The tube that carries the semen from the body is the _____. This tube also carries _____ from the bladder. Males can also have uncontrolled ejaculation during sleep, which are called _____ _____.

WHO'S WHO VOCABULARY WORKSHEET (SE-12)

DIRECTIONS: Read each word below and place an F if it is part of the female reproductive
system, an M if it is part of the male reproductive system, and a B if it is
part of both systems.

_____ 1. testosterone		_____16. Fallopian tubes
_____ 2. labia		_____17. nocturnal emission
_____ 3. sperm		_____18. estrogen
_____ 4. genitals		_____19. scrotum
_____ 5. pubic hair		_____20. ovulation
_____ 6. puberty		_____21. semen
_____ 7. ejaculation		_____22. erection
_____ 8. hormones		_____23. progesterone
_____ 9. ovaries		_____24. urethra
_____10. cervix		_____25. placenta
_____11. menstruation		_____26. foreskin
_____12. testes		_____27. hymen
_____13. vagina		_____28. prostate
_____14. bladder		_____29. clitoris
_____15. uterus		_____30. seminal vesicles

© 1993 by The Center for Applied Research in Education

Do I have that estrogen stuff or do you?

Name _____   **Date** _____

ANATOMY CHALLENGE (SE-13)

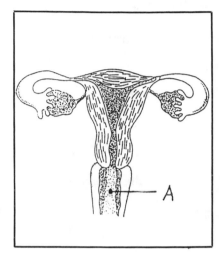
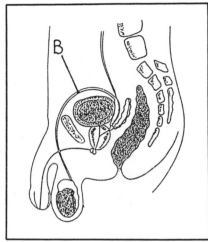
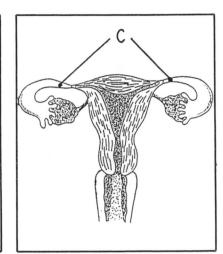

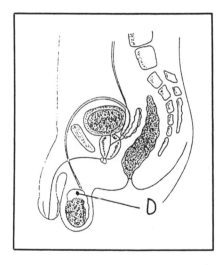
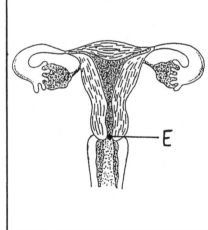
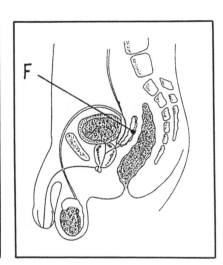

DIRECTIONS: Label each part of the reproductive system as it corresponds to the letter.

A. _____   D. _____

B. _____   E. _____

C. _____   F. _____

VOCABULARY CHALLENGE (SE-14)

DIRECTIONS: Place the correct letter in the blank to the left. Letters may be used only once.

_____ 1. testosterone	A. brings urine and semen out of body through the penis
_____ 2. fetus	B. adds a chemical fluid to the semen
_____ 3. semen	C. when the penis becomes engorged with blood and hard
_____ 4. fertilization	D. where fertilization takes place
_____ 5. erection	E. glands that produce the egg cells and hormones
_____ 6. prostate gland	F. first two months of development in the uterus
_____ 7. ovaries	G. organ that nourishes the fetus
_____ 8. egg cells	H. stores sperm cells
_____ 9. cervix	I. female organ of intercourse; birth canal
_____ 10. seminal vesicles	J. female erectile tissue between the labia
_____ 11. testes	K. houses the fetus during pregnancy
_____ 12. vas deferens	L. adds a sugary fluid to semen
_____ 13. ejaculation	M. folds of skin outside of the vagina
_____ 14. puberty	N. a hormone produced in the ovaries
_____ 15. scrotum	O. cells produced in the ovaries
_____ 16. vagina	P. cells produced in the testes
_____ 17. Fallopian tubes	Q. entrance to the uterus
_____ 18. embryo	R. when the semen leaves the penis
_____ 19. estrogen	S. fluid ejaculated from the penis
_____ 20. uterus	T. organ that produces sperm
_____ 21. labia	U. male hormone
_____ 22. epididymis	V. begins at about age 12 or 13
_____ 23. urethra	W. last 7 months of prenatal development
_____ 24. clitoris	X. tube that carries sperm from testes
_____ 25. sperm cells	Y. sperm cell joins egg cell
_____ 26. placenta	Z. sac that regulates the temperature of the testes

Name _____ Date _____

YOU'RE OUTTA HERE (SE-15)

DIRECTIONS: In each group, one item does not belong. Circle the item that does not belong and briefly explain why.

1.   ESTROGEN   PROGESTERONE   TESTOSTERONE

Why? _____

2.   AMOEBA   EMBRYO   FETUS

Why? _____

3.   THYMUS   AMNIOTIC SAC   PLACENTA

Why? _____

4.   FALLOPIAN TUBE   VAGINA   PROSTATE

Why? _____

5.   SEMINAL VESICLE   VAS DEFERENS   OVARIES

Why? _____

6.   URETHRA   BLADDER   TESTES

Why? _____

7.   CONDOM   TUBAL LIGATION   VASECTOMY

Why? _____

8.   TUBERCULOSIS   CHLAMYDIA   TRICHOMONIASIS

Why? _____

9.   1ST EJACULATION   MENOPAUSE   ONSET OF MENSTRUATION

Why? _____

10.   CERVIX   URETHRA   PROSTATE

Why? _____

REPRODUCTIVE SYSTEM: DISEASES & DISORDERS (SE-16)

DIRECTIONS: Choose the best answer by circling the correct letter.

1. A tear in the abdominal wall near the scrotum which may allow the intestines to push through is a(n):
   a. appendicitis
   b. inguinal hernia
   c. form of prostate cancer
2. The inability to reproduce because the sperm cells are unable to fertilize the egg is called:
   a. sterility
   b. impotence
   c. premature ejaculation
3. An abnormal growth of cells is called:
   a. mono
   b. hepatitis
   c. cancer

4. A common site of cancer in men is the:
   a. epididymis
   b. prostate
   c. Cowper's gland
5. A sign of testicular cancer is:
   a. nodules on the testes
   b. nausea
   c. a severe skin rash
6. A condition in which the inner lining of the uterus is present abnormally in the abdominal cavity is called:
   a. psychosis
   b. endometriosis
   c. scoliosis
7. Which is NOT a type of vaginitis?
   a. trichomoniasis
   b. yeast infection
   c. PMS
8. For which reason is a Pap smear given?
   a. to detect AIDS
   b. to detect cervical cancer
   c. to detect breast cancer
9. Which is NOT a cause of sterility?
   a. an untreated STD
   b. certain illnesses, such as mumps in an adult
   c. depression
10. Depression, mood swings, bloating, anxiety, and irritability are symptoms of:
    a. PMS
    b. breast cancer
    c. vaginitis

PREGNANCY AND CHILDBIRTH

- **Signs and Stages of Pregnancy**

- **Pregnancy and Childbirth**

SIGNS OF PREGNANCY (SE-17)

DIRECTIONS: Choose the best answer from the
list below and fill in the blanks.
The answers will be used only once.

SIGNS OF PREGNANCY

1. Period is _____ or missed.

2. Abnormal period, lighter or _____ than usual.

3. Breast _____ or fullness.

4. Nausea and sometimes _____.

5. Changes in _____.

6. Frequent _____.

7. Fatigue or _____.

PREGNANCY TESTS

1. URINE TEST—to detect the presence of _____, a hormone that
is produced when a woman is pregnant.

2. PELVIC EXAM—to check the _____ of the uterus.

3. BLOOD TEST—rarely used because _____ tests are
simpler to use and just as accurate.

| HCG | TENDERNESS | LATE | URINATION | APPETITE |
| SHORTER | VOMITING | SIZE | TIREDNESS | URINE |

© 1993 by The Center for Applied Research in Education

DEVELOPMENT OF THE EMBRYO AND FETUS (SE-18)

3-4 WEEKS

Called an EMBRYO
Heartbeat
Brain forming
1/4 inch long
Lungs forming

6 WEEKS

Fingers, toes
Ears
Skin forming

8 WEEKS

1-1/2 inches long
1/30 of an ounce
All organs have
   begun to develop

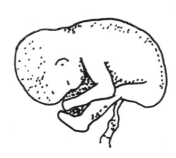

12 WEEKS

Now called a FETUS
Movement felt
3 inches long
Can swallow

9 MONTHS

19-21 inches long
Full term pregnancy
7-9 pounds
Organs can function
   on their own now

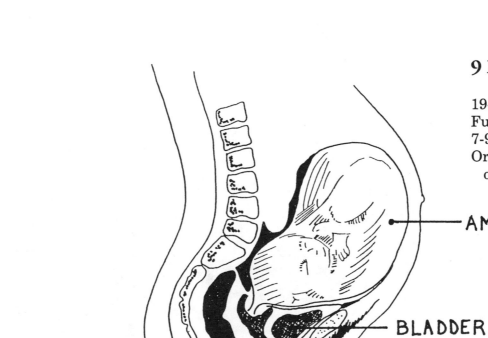

AMNIOTIC SAC

BLADDER

RECTUM

VAGINA

PREGNANCY AND CHILDBIRTH STAGES (SE-19)

DIRECTIONS: Number the stages of pregnancy and childbirth in the correct order.

EMBRYO is now called a FETUS.

Cells multiply to form the placenta.

The fertilized egg implants itself.

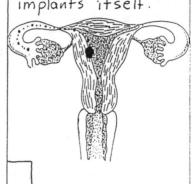

Pregnancy is full term.

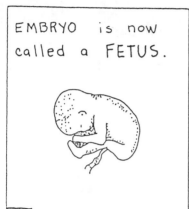

The egg cell and sperm cell join.

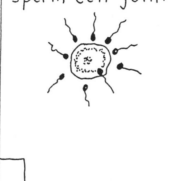

Baby is referred to as an EMBRYO.

Placenta and umbilical cord are pushed out.

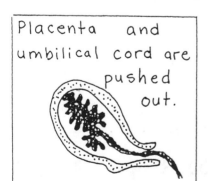

Labor: The cervix dilates to 10 cm.

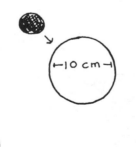

The baby is pushed out.

CHILDBIRTH CROSSWORD CHALLENGE (SE-20)

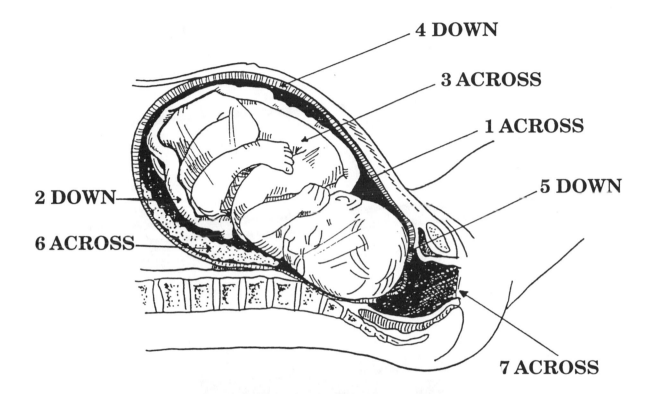

4 DOWN

3 ACROSS

1 ACROSS

5 DOWN

2 DOWN

6 ACROSS

7 ACROSS

CONTRACEPTION*

- **Contraception Terminology**

- **Chemical Methods of Contraception**

- **Mechanical Methods of Contraception**

- **Abstinence Methods of Contraception**

- **Permanent Methods of Contraception**

- **Contraceptive Comparison Discussion**

* Be sure to check your district policy or seek school board approval before teaching contraception or any other sex education topic.

CONTRACEPTIVE MATCH-UP (SE-21)

a. DIAPHRAGM   b. pill   C. I.U.D.   d. RHYTHM

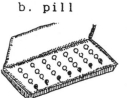
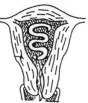

e. CONDOM   f. FOAM/JELLY   g. SPONGE   h. CERVICAL CAP

© 1993 by The Center for Applied Research in Education

DIRECTIONS: Match the picture with the correct statement by placing the letters in the blank to the left of each statement. Letters may be used more than once.

_____ 1. Rubber sheath placed over the penis.

_____ 2. Abstinence during ovulation.

_____ 3. Used with jelly to block the sperm from entering the uterus.

_____ 4. Prevents ovulation.

_____ 5. An over-the-counter sperm barrier that is used with spermicide.

_____ 6. If treated with nonoxynol 9, this method also helps prevent the spread of STDs.

_____ 7. Inserted into the uterus by a physician.

_____ 8. May cause initial weight gain and is dangerous to women over 35 who smoke.

_____ 9. Blocks the entrance to the uterus by fitting directly over the cervix.

_____ 10. A method of birth control considered unsafe for young girls and many women.

CHEMICAL METHODS OF CONTRACEPTION (SE-22)

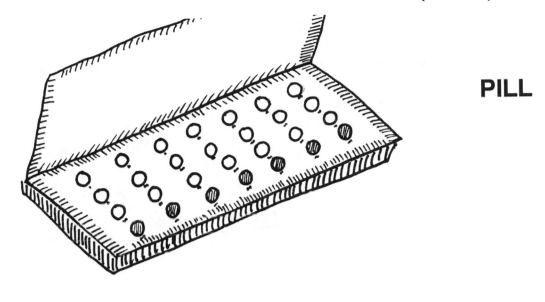

PILL

Description: _____

_____

_____

_____

Effectiveness %: _____
How do you obtain this? _____

_____

Possible side effects: _____

_____

_____

_____

Other: _____

_____

_____

_____

CHEMICAL METHODS OF CONTRACEPTION (SE-23)

VAGINAL SUPPOSITORIES

Description: _____
_____
_____
_____

Effectiveness %: _____
How do you obtain this? _____
_____

Possible side effects: _____
_____
_____

Other: _____
_____
_____
_____

CHEMICAL METHODS OF CONTRACEPTION (SE-24)

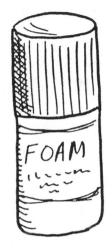

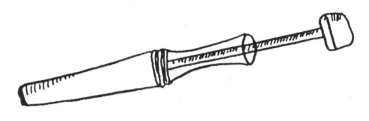

SPERMICIDAL FOAMS, JELLIES, CREAMS

Description: _____

_____

_____

_____

Effectiveness %: _____
How do you obtain this? _____

_____

Possible side effects: _____

_____

_____

Other: _____

_____

_____

_____

CHEMICAL METHODS OF CONTRACEPTION (SE-25)

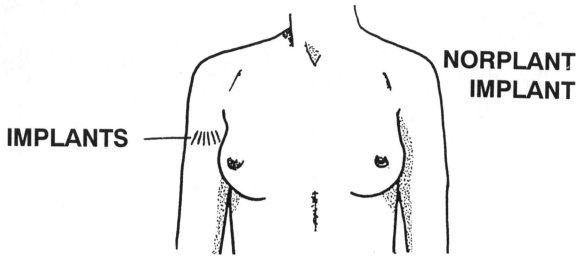

NORPLANT IMPLANT

IMPLANTS

Description: _____

_____

_____

_____

Effectiveness %: _____

How do you obtain this? _____

_____

_____

Possible side effects: _____

_____

_____

_____

Other: _____

_____

_____

_____

© 1993 by The Center for Applied Research in Education

MECHANICAL METHODS OF CONTRACEPTION (SE-26)

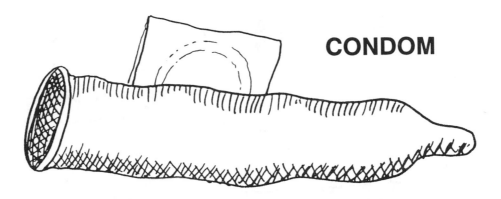

CONDOM

Description: _____

_____

_____

_____

Effectiveness %: _____

How do you obtain this? _____

_____

Possible side effects: _____

_____

_____

_____

Other: _____

_____

_____

_____

MECHANICAL METHODS OF CONTRACEPTION (SE-27)

DIAPHRAGM

Description: _____
_____
_____
_____

Effectiveness %: _____
How do you obtain this? _____
_____

Possible side effects: _____
_____
_____
_____

Other: _____
_____
_____
_____

MECHANICAL METHODS OF CONTRACEPTION (SE-28)

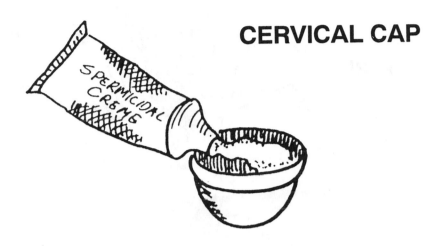

CERVICAL CAP

Description: _____

_____

_____

_____

Effectiveness %: _____

How do you obtain this? _____

_____

Possible side effects: _____

_____

_____

_____

Other: _____

_____

_____

_____

MECHANICAL METHODS OF CONTRACEPTION (SE-29)

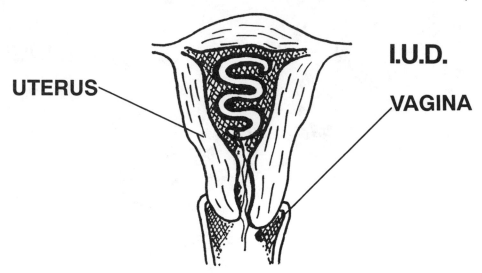

UTERUS

I.U.D.

VAGINA

Description: _____
_____
_____
_____

Effectiveness %: _____
How do you obtain this? _____
_____

Possible side effects: _____
_____
_____
_____

Other: _____
_____
_____
_____

MECHANICAL METHODS OF CONTRACEPTION (SE-30)

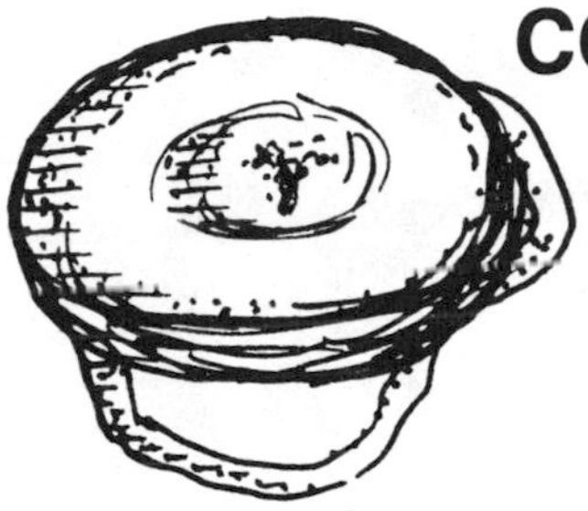

CONTRACEPTIVE SPONGE

Description: _____

_____

_____

_____

Effectiveness %: _____

How do you obtain this? _____

_____

Possible side effects: _____

_____

_____

_____

Other: _____

_____

_____

_____

ABSTINENCE METHODS OF CONTRACEPTION (SE-31)

ABSTINENCE

Description: _____
_____
_____
_____

Effectiveness %: _____
How do you obtain this? _____
_____

Possible side effects: _____
_____
_____
_____

Other: _____
_____
_____
_____

ABSTINENCE METHODS OF CONTRACEPTION (SE-32)

WITHDRAWAL

Description: _____

_____

_____

_____

Effectiveness %: _____

How do you obtain this? _____

_____

Possible side effects: _____

_____

_____

_____

Other: _____

_____

_____

_____

ABSTINENCE METHODS OF CONTRACEPTION (SE-33)

FEBRUARY 2014

RHYTHM

Description: _____
_____
_____
_____

Effectiveness %: _____
How do you obtain this? _____
_____
_____

Possible side effects: _____
_____
_____
_____

Other: _____
_____
_____
_____

PERMANENT METHODS OF CONTRACEPTION (SE-34)

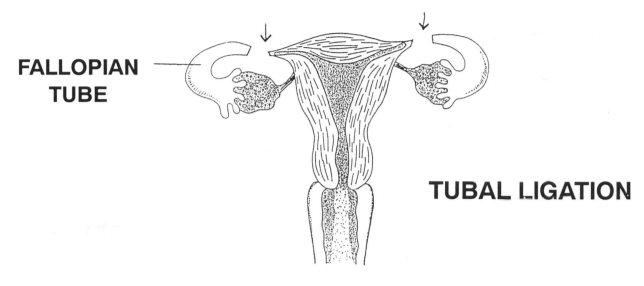

FALLOPIAN TUBE

TUBAL LIGATION

Description: _____

_____

_____

_____

Effectiveness %: _____

How do you obtain this? _____

_____

_____

Possible side effects: _____

_____

_____

_____

Other: _____

_____

_____

_____

PERMANENT METHODS OF CONTRACEPTION (SE-35)

VAS DEFERENS

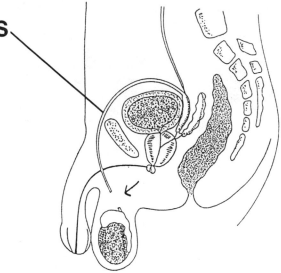

VASECTOMY

Description: _____

_____

_____

_____

Effectiveness %: _____

How do you obtain this? _____

_____

_____

Possible side effects: _____

_____

_____

_____

Other: _____

_____

_____

_____

ACTIVITY 2: WHAT'S THE DIFFERENCE?
(Contraceptive comparison and discussion)

Concept/ Description: Students are frequently misinformed about contraception.

Objective: Students will compare and discuss the effectiveness, side effects, cost, and methods of use of various birth control products.

Materials: Contraceptive products, such as:

condom	sponge
diaphragm	pills
I.U.D.	cervical cap
foam, jelly	

copies of Contraception Comparison Chart (see SE-36)

pen or pencil

Note: Many products are available over-the-counter, from a gynecologist, or from family planning centers. Complete teaching kits are often available on loan from some family planning centers as well.

Directions:
1. Hand out the Contraception Comparison Charts.
2. As you show the actual product, or diagram, explain how it works, and have students fill in the chart accordingly.
3. Categorize the methods into Chemical, Mechanical, Abstinence and Permanent (surgical).
4. Compare the side effects, effectiveness, and approximate cost.
5. List the methods from least to most effective.
6. Discuss the factors that would prevent a young person from using birth control, such as embarrassment, religious beliefs, lack of knowledge, too much trouble, etc.
7. Ask if students feel that young people would have difficulty talking to their partner about birth control. Why or why not?
8. If someone is too uncomfortable to discuss birth control and the consequences of intercourse without protection, are they mature enough to be having sex? Discuss.

Name _____ Date _____

CONTRACEPTION COMPARISON CHART (SE-36)

METHOD	CATEGORY	HOW IT WORKS	SIDE EFFECTS	% OF EFFECTIVE-NESS	COST

SEXUALLY TRANSMITTED DISEASES

- **STD Signs, Symptoms, and Solutions**

- **AIDS**

STD SYMPTOMS SEEK 'N FIND (SE-37)

c	c	i	t	a	m	o	t	p	m	y	s	a	a
t	l	d	i	s	c	h	a	r	g	e	r	e	l
o	e	h	s	o	p	h	m	m	e	e	e	t	s
s	e	r	o	s	d	i	a	r	t	g	o	l	y
c	d	r	a	a	i	v	w	a	x	n	q	j	k
s	i	v	r	s	d	d	u	e	o	i	b	e	g
b	f	v	w	s	h	a	g	h	c	n	t	i	r
p	e	r	l	w	u	e	r	r	r	r	r	f	b
d	t	y	i	e	n	t	s	r	n	u	v	m	o
x	i	p	r	i	p	s	v	a	b	b	g	t	e
f	f	a	t	i	g	u	e	i	u	i	o	n	c
p	e	a	s	w	q	u	n	d	r	t	e	z	i
d	l	f	i	g	n	i	h	c	t	i	i	r	s
s	u	s	a	m	e	r	i	g	o	l	k	d	o

DIRECTIONS: Find ten words dealing with STD symptoms in the puzzle above. Words may be forward, backward, vertical, horizontal, or diagonal. Use the clues given to determine the words used.

CLUES:

A type of skin change.
Occurs when urinating.
Pus from the penis or vagina.
Another type of skin change.
Loose, watery stools.
Tiredness.
Having no symptoms.
Severe pain in this area.
Occurs around genitals.
Another name for reproductive organs.

```
                                       S
                            _ _ _ _ _ I   G
                        _ I _ _ _ _ R _ _
                                    O _ _
                            _ _ R R _ _ _
                            F _ _ _ _ _ E
                A S _ _ _ _ _ _ _ _ _ _ C
                            _ _ _ _ V _
                        I _ _ _ I _
                        E _ _ T _ _
```

Name _____ **Date** _____

STD FACT CHART (SE-38)

Disease	Pathogen	Where	How	Symptoms
AIDS				
Chlamydia				
Genital Herpes				
Syphilis				

DIRECTIONS: For each disease listed on the chart, fill in the *pathogen* that causes it, *where* it enters the human body, *how* it enters the human body, and the *symptoms* that are characteristic of the disease.

Name _____   Date _____

STD FACT CHART (SE-39)

Disease	Pathogen	Where	How	Symptoms
Gonorrhea				
Genital Warts				
Hepatitis				
Non-Gonococ-cal Urethritis (NGU)				

1993 by The Center for Applied Research in Education

DIRECTIONS: For each disease listed on the chart, fill in the *pathogen* that causes it, *where* it enters the human body, *how* it enters the human body, and the *symptoms* that are characteristic of the disease.

48

Name _____   **Date** _____

STD FACT CHART (SE-40)

Disease	Pathogen	Where	How	Symptoms
Vaginitis				
Pubic Lice				
Trichomoniasis				
Scabies				

DIRECTIONS: For each disease listed on the chart, fill in the *pathogen* that causes it, *where* it enters the human body, *how* it enters the human body, and the *symptoms* that are characteristic of the disease.

WAYS TO AVOID STD'S (SE-41)

NO SEX

BEST WAY

Next Best

**Ways to
Reduce the
Chances**

FIDELITY:
ONE PARTNER

USE A CONDOM
W/ NONOXYNOL-9

SELECT PARTNER
CAREFULLY

WASH AFTER
SEX

URINATE AFTER
SEX

USE FOAM OR
JELLY WITH A
CONDOM.

GET REGULAR
STD CHECK-UPS.

STDS: GETTING HELP (SE-42)

1. Call the AIDS National Hotline:
   1-800-342-AIDS (toll free)
2. Call the VD National Hotline:
   1-800-227-8922 (toll free)

3. Call area clinics: _____

   _____

   _____

4. Call the Department of Health: _____

   _____

   _____

NOTE: If you are under 18, the law permits you to obtain confidential STD medical care without parental permission. It is, however, suggested that you consult with your parents if at all possible.

Name _____ **Date** _____

AIDS/STD CROSSWORD CHALLENGE (SE-43)

Clues

Across
1. A protein that fights off foreign substances.
4. A type of sarcoma that AIDS patients develop.
6. The first test given to determine the presence of the HIV.
7. One of the main ways STD's and AIDS is spread. (2 words)
10. AIDS is NOT spread through _____ contact, such as hugging or kissing.
12. A type of pneumonia that AIDS patients develop.
14. An STD characterized by open sores known as chancres.
15. An STD characterized by intense itching and nits attached to the pubic hair. (2 words)
16. The type of pathogen that causes AIDS.
18. An STD that is caused by bacteria that lives in the warm, moist areas of the body and is one of the most common communicable diseases.
19. A common inflammation of the vagina.
20. An incurable virus that causes blister-

ing sores in the genital area.
21. The fluid ejaculated from the penis.

Down
2. A vaginal infection that is caused by a protozoan parasite.
3. The type of lymphocytes that produce antibodies. (2 words)
5. A microorganism that causes infectious diseases.
8. A body fluid that is present in the mouth and does not transmit the AIDS virus.
9. When intravenous drug users share _____, AIDS can be transmitted.
11. The only sure way to avoid AIDS and STD's.
13. The body's ability to fight off harmful substances.
17. A condition in which mites burrow under the skin.

WHAT IS AIDS? (SE-44)

DIRECTIONS: Fill in the missing letters to give an accurate explanation of AIDS.

The __ __ M __ __ immunodeficiency V __ __ __ __ is the pathogen that causes

__ I __ __. AIDS stands for acquired __ __ __ __ N __ deficiency

S __ __ R __ __ __. Though the virus is very powerful, it cannot live

O __ __ __ __ __ E the human body. It does live in certain body fluids, such as

__ __ O __ __, __ __ M __ __, and __ __ G __ __ L secretions.

AIDS is spread through sexual __ __ __ __ R C __ __ __ __ __—oral,

A __ __ __, or vaginal. It is also spread by using contaminated __ E E __ __ __ __,

receiving a blood __ __ __ N __ __ __ __ __ __ N with contaminated blood or blood

products, or it is passed from an AIDS-infected __ __ T __ __ __ to her C __ __ __ __

before birth.

The best prevention against infection is __ __ __ T __ __ E __ __ __, which is

not having sex. If a person does have sex, then the relationship should be

M __ __ __ __ __ __ __ __ __ S , having only one partner. If a person chooses the dangerous

practice of having more than one partner, then the Surgeon General recommends the use of a

__ __ __ __ O __ .

There is no known __ U __ __ for AIDS at the present time. Any person who contracts

AIDS will die.

THE HEALTHY IMMUNE SYSTEM (SE-45)

DIRECTIONS: Fill in the blanks using the words below to explain how the healthy immune system functions.

VIRUS	BACTERIA	ILLNESS	ANTIBODIES
NORMAL	ANTIBIOTICS	MULTIPLIES	IMMUNE
T-CELLS	B-CELLS	WHITE BLOOD CELLS	
CHEMICALLY	PROTOZOAN	FUNGI	

1. A germ (_____ , _____ ,

_____ , _____ , etc.) invades the body and

quickly _____ .

2. The healthy _____ system fights back by sending

_____ to destroy the invaders.

3. First, the _____ surround and "eat" some

of the invaders, then _____ notify the

4. _____ which, in turn, produce

5. _____ which destroy the germs.

6. Germs that survive the attack can cause _____ .

7. _____ help to finally destroy all the germs.

8. _____ health is restored.

54

Name _____ **Date** _____

AIDS-INFECTED IMMUNE SYSTEM (SE-46)

DIRECTIONS: Fill in the blanks using the words below to explain what happens to the AIDS infected immune system.

KAPOSI'S	B-CELLS	"FACTORIES"	ATTACHES
T-CELLS	HIV	CANNOT	ANTIBODIES
DESTROYED	DIE	PNEUMONIA	OPPORTUNISTIC
DEMENTIA			

1. The _____ invades the body and quickly multiplies.

2. The immune system tries to fight back by sending white blood cells to destroy the invaders.

3. _____ surround and attempt to "eat" the HIV,

4. but the HIV _____ itself to the T-cells causing

them to become HIV-producing _____.

5. The T-cells _____ chemically notify

the _____ , and therefore,

6. the _____ cannot produce _____.

7. The immune system is _____ and the person is susceptible to

many _____ diseases, such as:

8. Pneumocystis carinii _____, _____

sarcoma, and AIDS _____ complex.

9. These diseases usually cause the person to _____.

HOW AIDS IS SPREAD (SE-47)

1. SEX: _____
_____
_____

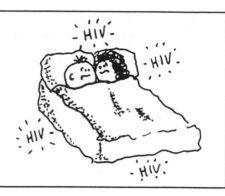

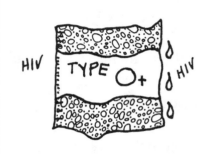

2. Blood transfusion with _____ blood or blood products.

© 1993 by The Center for Applied Research in Education

3. Using contaminated IV drug _____.

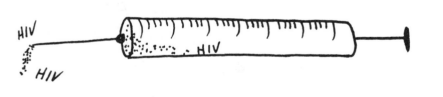

4. From _____ to baby at birth.

Name _____ **Date** _____

HOW AIDS IS NOT SPREAD (SE-48)

1. __ __ __ __ __ __ __

2. **sharing the same**
__ __ __ __ __ __ __ __
facilities

3. __ __ __ __ __ __ __
such as mosquitoes

4. __ __ __ __ __ __ __
blood

5. **getting a** __ __ __ __ __ __ __   __ __ __ __

6. __ __ __ __ __ __ __ __ **hands**

7. **sharing eating** __ __ __ __ __ __

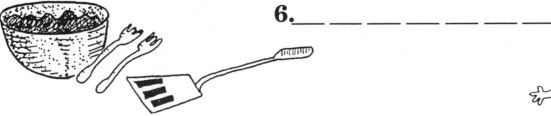

57

HOW THE AIDS VIRUS CAN AFFECT YOU (SE-49)

DIRECTIONS: Using the words in the answer key, write the best answer in the blank.

HOW THE AIDS VIRUS CAN AFFECT YOU:

1. *Asymptomatic*

   You could have the HIV in your body and have no _____ or

   _____. You could appear _____

   but still pass the disease to others.

2. *ARC (AIDS Related Complex)*

   A person infected with the HIV could have some _____ symptoms

   of AIDS, such as fatigue, diarrhea, _____, swollen lymph

   nodes, loss of _____, weight loss, skin

   _____, and night _____.

3. *AIDS*

   This is developed 6 months to 10 years after infection. Once you have AIDS you will live

   from 6 months to 3 years. AIDS patients usually die of an

   _____ _____, such as

   pneumocystis carinii pneumonia, Kaposi's sarcoma, or AIDS dementia complex. People

   with healthy immune systems do not get these diseases.

TO AVOID AIDS:

1. Practice abstinence—no _____.
2. Practice monogamy—one _____.
3. Use a _____ treated with nonoxynol-9.
4. Don't use illegal IV drugs and don't share _____.
5. Don't share objects that get _____ on them, such as razors or
   toothbrushes.

BLOOD	NEEDLES	CONDOM	EARLY	SEX
HEALTHY	PARTNER	RASHES	APPETITE	FEVER
SWEATS	SYMPTOMS	SIGNS	OPPORTUNISTIC	DISEASE

© 1993 by The Center for Applied Research in Education

AIDS TRUE/FALSE WORKSHEET (SE-50)

DIRECTIONS: On the line to the left, write T if the statement is true. If the statement is not true, replace the underlined words with words that would make the statement true.

_____ 1. The HIV is most likely to attack the B cells.

_____ 2. Antibodies are proteins that destroy foreign substances.

_____ 3. The first test given to determine the presence of AIDS antibodies is the

Western Blot test.

_____ 4. AIDS is caused by a fungus.

_____ 5. Being protected from disease means you are immune.

_____ 6. Having one sexual partner is called bigamy.

_____ 7. A heterosexual has sexual partners of both sexes.

_____ 8. HIV is found in the highest concentrations in blood, vaginal secretions,

and urine.

_____ 9. The best way to avoid getting AIDS is using a condom.

_____10. AIDS destroys the body's digestive system, leaving the victim susceptible

to other diseases.

ACTIVITY 3: WHAT ARE YOU GONNA DO? (AIDS Dilemmas)

Concept/
Description: It is important to understand that there are many difficult situations a person with AIDS faces.

Objective: Students will be asked to think through and discuss situations dealing with AIDS and how they might react.

Materials: Copies of What Are You Gonna Do? sheets (SE-51 – SE-55)
Pens or pencils

Directions: 1. Give each student a sheet and have them read each situation and write down their immediate responses.
2. Discuss each dilemma as a class.
3. Allow students to change their responses after discussion, if they wish.

Variations: 1. Assign groups to discuss specific dilemmas.
2. Assign each group a "secretary" who will jot down the group's feelings and a "spokesperson" who will report the feelings back to the class.

"What am I gonna do?"

WHAT ARE YOU GONNA DO? (SE-51)
(AIDS Dilemmas)

DIRECTIONS: Read each situation and answer the questions in the area provided.

Dilemma 1: Your best friend, who frequently stays at your house, has a positive result on the AIDS antibody test.

- How would this make you feel?

- Would you continue to be friends with this person?

- Would your relationship change?

- Why or why not? Explain.

WHAT ARE YOU GONNA DO? (SE-52)
(AIDS Dilemmas)

DIRECTIONS: Read each situation and answer the questions in the area provided.

Dilemma 2: Your eight-year-old son plays with a boy who has just been diagnosed as having AIDS. They usually are very rough when they play.

- As a parent, would you allow them to continue to play together?

- Would you put restrictions on the way that they play? If so, what restrictions?

- What would you say to your son?

- Why would you say that?

WHAT ARE YOU GONNA DO? (SE-53)
(AIDS Dilemmas)

DIRECTIONS: Read each situation and answer the questions in the area provided.

Dilemma 3: A woman who owns a very successful restaurant fires her chef because he has AIDS. The fired chef takes the woman to court. You are the judge.

- What would you do or say?

- Why do you feel that way?

- Should the owner be forced to rehire the chef?

- Even if having that chef kept people away from the restaurant, should the woman be forced to rehire him?

Hmmmm... What would I do?

WHAT ARE YOU GONNA DO? (SE-54)
(AIDS Dilemmas)

DIRECTIONS: Read each situation and answer the questions in the area provided.

Dilemma 4: You have a positive result on the AIDS antibody test but you don't have any of the signs or symptoms. Your boyfriend/girlfriend wants to have a more serious relationship and you are very much in love.

• How would you feel? Would you tell him/her?

• Would you continue the relationship?

• What would you do or what would you say to him/her?

• Why?

WHAT ARE YOU GONNA DO? (SE-55)
(AIDS Dilemmas)

DIRECTIONS: Read each situation and answer the questions in the area provided.

Dilemma 5: Your best friend's boyfriend has cheated on her several times. When you tried to tell her about it, she became angry at you and accused you of just being jealous. Recently, you found out that one of the girls he was with has AIDS.

- Would you tell your best friend and risk your friendship?

- Why do you feel this way?

- If you told her, what would you say?

- How would you feel if your friend contracted AIDS and you didn't tell her?

SEXUAL DECISION MAKING AND TOPICS FOR DISCUSSION

- **Teen Pregnancy Options**

- **Consequences of Intercourse Before Marriage**

- **Skits and Raps**

- **Sex Education Discussion Questions**

- **Analyzing Songs Dealing With Sex**

- **Research Questions for Discussion**

- **Practicing Refusal Skills**

ACTIVITY 4: IT'S UP TO YOU
(Teen Pregnancy Options)

Concept/ Description: If a couple decides to have unprotected sex and pregnancy results, there are several options available.

Objective: To have students consider the options available if teen pregnancy occurs.

Materials: Teen Pregnancy Options Sheet (SE-56)
Pen or pencil

Directions: 1. Distribute the Teen Pregnancy Options Sheet.
2. Ask students to discuss the options available to an unwed mother and further discuss the pros and cons.
3. Have students fill in the sheet according to their individual beliefs and prepare to discuss as a class.

Variation: Have students debate their choices.

TEEN PREGNANCY OPTIONS (SE-56)

1. Keep baby: Marriage

PROS _____

_____

_____

CONS _____

_____

_____

2. Keep baby: Unmarried

PROS _____

_____

_____

CONS _____

_____

_____

3. Have baby: Adoption

PROS _____

_____

_____

CONS _____

_____

_____

4. Abortion

PROS _____

_____

_____

CONS _____

_____

_____

ACTIVITY 5: LET'S TALK ABOUT SEX
(Consequences of Intercourse Before Marriage)

"I'm not ready for this...."

Concept/ Description: If a person chooses to have sex before marriage, there are consequences that must be considered.

Objective: To have students list all the possible questions they must ask themselves before having sex.

Materials: None.

Directions:
1. Divide students into groups and have them brainstorm questions that they must ask themselves before having sex.
2. Bring the groups back together as a class and ask each group to write one of their questions on the board.
3. List as many questions as the class can think of.
4. Discuss.

Examples:
1. Do I want to have kids?
2. If not, will I use birth control?
3. If so, what is available?
4. What are the side effects of each method?
5. Where will I get contraception?
6. How much will it cost?
7. Where will I get the money?
8. If pregnancy results, will we get married?
9. Will we have the baby?
10. Will the baby be put up for adoption?
11. How will we tell our parents?
12. Will she have an abortion?
13. Where is an abortion performed?
14. How much does it cost?
15. Am I opposed to abortion?
16. What if I get a sexually transmitted disease?
17. How will I know? What are the signs?
18. How can I be treated?
19. Where can I get treatment?
20. What if I get AIDS?

ACTIVITY 6: THINGS THAT MAKE YOU GO HMMMMMM...
(Skits or Raps)

Concept/ Description: It will be necessary for students to research material in order to be able to make a skit or rap.

Objective: Students will make up a skit or rap on the topic of their choice. Each skit or rap must include eight to ten facts about the topic.

Materials: Will vary with each group.

Directions:
1. Divide students into groups of four or five.
2. Each group is to come up with a skit or rap depicting their feelings about a particular topic that has been discussed in class. For example, topics could include teen pregnancy, birth control, and saying no.
3. Add any parameter that you feel your class would need to keep the project in good taste.
4. Groups must present a written script before performing for the class.
5. Allow the groups to perform for the class (videotape if possible) or have the best groups perform for other classes.
6. Evaluation could be done by the teacher or by the other members of the class.

"And now, I'd like to say...."

ACTIVITY 7: I HEARD THAT!
(Fishbowl Class Discussion)

Concept/ Description: Group discussions help students to broaden their views on controversial subjects. Being observed and critiqued while in a discussion can help students to develop better communication skills.

Objective: To observe and be observed in a group discussion.

Materials: Topics Sheet (see SE-57)
Dittoed Fishbowl Observation Sheets (see SE-58)
Pens or pencils

Directions:
1. Divide the class in half.
2. Arrange the chairs or desks in a circle-within-a-circle format, being certain that there are an equal number of chairs in each circle.
3. Have students take a seat and hand everyone in the outer circle a Fishbowl Observation Sheet.
4. The outside circle is to observe the person sitting in front of them, and check off columns as they apply.
5. The inside circle will discuss a topic chosen from the Topics Sheet or a topic assigned by the teacher.
   Note: The outside circle may not join in on the discussion no matter how tempting it may be. Their only job is to observe their partner.
6. When the discussion time limit has expired, have the observer and their "partner" discuss the findings.
7. As the teacher, you may wish to make some observations of your own such as, "John took over right from the start . . . did you feel comfortable doing that, John?" or "Kristen didn't say much, but her body language indicated to me that she was interested in the discussion."
8. Switch inside and outside groups, pass out the Fishbowl Observation Sheets to the outside group, and assign a new topic. Repeat the process.

FISHBOWL CLASS DISCUSSION TOPICS (SE-57)

1. Who should be told if a school-age child has AIDS? Should the nurse, teachers, administration, students, PE teachers, etc., know? Why or why not? Explain.

2. What would you do if you have a positive AIDS antibody test? How would you live your life?

3. Why do you think having an STD carries a stigma, when contracting other communicable diseases, such as the flu and chicken pox, does not? Do you think this stigma has an effect on whether someone seeks treatment? Explain.

4. Do you think it is morally and ethically acceptable to be a surrogate mother? In your opinion, does that mother have any rights to the child? Why or why not?

5. Should abortion be legal? Should a girl be able to get an abortion without her parent's permission? Why or why not?

6. Should homosexuals be barred from any type of profession, such as teacher, counselor, soldier, daycare worker? Why or why not?

7. What factors in teenage marriages contribute to a higher divorce rate than in marriages at an older age?

8. What special problems does a divorced parent face? What special problems do children of divorced parents face? How are grandparents and families affected?

9. Does advertising exploit sex to sell a product? Give examples and explain. What category of products uses sex to sell most often? (perfumes, jeans and other clothing items) Do you think it works? Why or why not?

10. Do you think condoms should be available in school? Why or why not? What problems might result, if any?

Name _____ **Date** _____

FISHBOWL OBSERVATION SHEET (SE-58)

Your Name _____

Person Being Observed _____

	1	2
1. Does the person give ideas or make suggestions?		
2. Does the student joke around or ease tension by laughing?		
3. Does the person agree with others? (shake head, state agreement, etc.)		
4. Does the person help others to explain what they mean?		
5. Does the person express his or her feelings or opinions?		
6. Does the person ask questions?		
7. Does the person ask other people their opinion?		
8. Does the person withdraw from the group?		
9. Does the person disagree with others a lot?		
10. Does the person put down people or make sarcastic comments?		

Name _____ **Date** _____

SEX IN ADVERTISING (SE-59)

DIRECTIONS: Cut out an advertisement in which "sex" is used to sell a product. Answer the questions below as they pertain to your ad. (Examples: perfume ads, liquor ads, clothing ads, suntan lotion ads)

1. What product is being sold?
_____
_____

2. Describe the physical background (setting) of your ad if there is one.
_____
_____
_____
_____

3. Describe the people in your ad.
_____
_____
_____
_____

4. Is any factual information about the product given? If so, what?
_____
_____
_____
_____

5. What image or message is the advertiser trying to get across with this ad?
_____
_____
_____
_____

6. According to the advertiser, what will this product supposedly do for you?
_____
_____
_____
_____

7. Why do you think "sex" was used to sell this product?
_____
_____
_____
_____

ACTIVITY 8: GIMME A BEAT!
(Analyzing Songs Dealing With Sex)

Concept/ Description: There are many songs that directly or indirectly send messages concerning sex.

Objective: Students will analyze various songs to determine if they give a positive or negative message concerning sex.

Materials: Tapes or CDs of various songs with sexual overtones
Tape or CD player
Copies of the words to the songs
Song Analysis Sheet (see SE-60)
(allow one sheet for each song per person, or group)
NOTE: The students themselves may be able to suggest and bring in the songs. They may also be willing to write out the words for you to copy.

Some Song Suggestions:
"Nasty" by Janet Jackson
"Do You Want Me?" by Salt 'n Pepa
"Let's Talk About Sex" by Salt 'n Pepa
"I Wanna Sex You Up" by Color Me Badd
"Straight Up" by Paula Abdul
"I Want Your Sex" by George Michael

Directions:
1. Hand out copies of the Song Analysis Sheet and the words to the songs.
2. Play a song and have students read along as the music is playing.
3. Ask individuals (or groups) to analyze each song and fill in their answers to each question.
4. Discuss.

Variation: Give this activity as a homework assignment. Ask each student to write out the words to a song and attach them to their completed Song Analysis Sheet.

Name _____ **Date** _____

SONG ANALYSIS SHEET (SE-60)

1. Is sex mentioned directly or indirectly in the song? Give an example.

   _____

   _____

   _____

   _____

2. Does the song suggest or promote pre-marital sex in any way? Explain.

   _____

   _____

   _____

   _____

3. Does the song mention sex in a loving relationship, or is there no mention of love? Explain or give an example.

   _____

   _____

   _____

   _____

4. What is the message you get from this song?

   _____

   _____

   _____

   _____

5. Do you think this song sends a positive or negative message concerning relationships? Why? Explain.

   _____

   _____

   _____

   _____

ACTIVITY 9: WHATTAYA KNOW?
(Research Questions for Discussion)

Concept/
Description: Students discover information through their own research and report back to the class.

Objective: To find out the answers to the questions through research (which may include interviews, telephone calls, visits to health centers and speaking to health professionals) and to report the findings to the class.

Materials: Copies of Research Questions Sheet (see SE-61)
Scissors

Directions:
1. Reproduce the Research Questions Sheet and cut out the boxes.
2. Place the pieces of paper in a container or hat and ask individual students (or groups) to choose one piece of paper.
3. Students are to find the answer to the questions and prepare a brief report to bring back to the class.
4. Ask individuals (or groups) to discuss their questions.

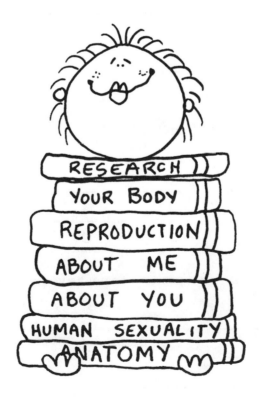

RESEARCH QUESTIONS (SE-61)

What is a hysterectomy? Why is it done? Explain.	What is *in vitro* fertilization? Explain.	Can a woman have children if she has one ovary? Explain.
What is surrogate parenting? Explain.	What is artificial insemination? Explain.	What is a miscarriage? What are some causes?
Do identical twins share the same placenta? Amniotic sac?	Can a man father children if the prostate gland is removed?	What is toxic shock syndrome? Explain.
What is menopause? When does it occur?	What dangers are associated with taking artificial steroids?	What is premature ejaculation? Explain.
Does a woman who has had a partial hysterectomy still menstruate?	What is impotence? Why may it occur? Explain.	What is endometriosis? How is it treated?
What is a Pap smear? Why is it given? Explain.	What is a Caesarean section? Why is it done? Explain.	What is an OB/GYN? What does one do? Explain.
What is the difference between identical and fraternal twins?	What are some common signs of labor? Explain.	What is a D&C and what do the letters stand for? Explain.

HOW TO SAY "NO" AND STILL BE FRIENDS (SE-62)

These are some suggestions for saying "No" and still keeping your friends. Practice them with a partner.

1. Know ahead of time how you feel about something such as sex, drugs, smoking, or drinking.

2. Be friendly, but be firm. Repeat to your friend what he or she has said to you. "You want me to have sex with you?"

3. Say how you honestly feel. Don't lie or you may be forced to make up more lies to cover up the first one. "At this time in my life, I don't feel comfortable with that."

4. Speak only for yourself rather than for everyone else. "I'm not ready to have sex yet."

5. Discuss the possible consequences. "If I were to get pregnant, it would ruin my chance to go to college."

6. Separate the activity from the person and let your friend know you care for him or her, but feel uncomfortable about the activity. "I really do care about you, but I can't take this risk."

7. Suggest an alternative. "Let's just go out for a while and walk along the beach."

8. If the person persists, walk away from the situation, but leave the "door open" for him or her to join you. "I'm going to take a walk. I'll be at the dock for a while, and I hope you'll meet me there."

9. Be prepared to accept the fact that you may be rejected no matter how nice you try to be.

© 1993 by The Center for Applied Research in Education

ACTIVITY 10: PRESSURE POINTS
(Practicing Refusal Skills)

Concept/ Learning to say no when you
Description: mean no is difficult for
teenagers when pressured
by peers.

Uhhh .....
I ... uh...
Well ...
I don't think
er ... I ... uh ...

Objective: To practice using refusal skills
in situations dealing with sex.

Materials: Pressure Cards (see SE-63)

Directions: 1. Cut the Pressure Cards apart and pass them out to volunteers.
(Laminate the cards if desired.)
2. Choose one of the volunteers and assign him or her a partner of the
opposite sex.
3. In front of the class, have the person with the card attempt to pressure
the partner using the "line" written on the card.
4. After each situation is acted out, discuss the "line" and ask what might
be the best response.
5. Other questions for discussion:

- Do you think it is more difficult for a guy to refuse a girl, or
vice versa? Why?
- Do you think guys would refuse girls? Why or why not?
- Do you think kids at this school would make fun of someone
who refuses a "popular" person?
- What are some reasons a young person might want to wait
before having intercourse?

PRESSURE CARDS (SE-63)

This is ridiculous! We're the only ones not having sex!	What's wrong with you? Are you a prude or something?
Don't you trust me? I would never do anything to hurt our relationship.	This will bring us so much closer. If you love me, we'll do this.
We've been dating for so long. What are we waiting for?	If this is the way you really feel, I guess there's no reason to keep dating.

© 1993 by The Center for Applied Research in Education

STOP

GENERAL REVIEW ACTIVITIES

ACTIVITY 11: BINGO!
(Sex Education Vocabulary Bingo)

Concept/ Description: Bingo is an enjoyable way to learn the numerous vocabulary words dealing with the reproductive systems.

Objective: Students will become familiar with the vocabulary words by attempting to get "bingo" and win the game.

Materials: Copied Blank Bingo Cards (see SE-64)
Copied Sex Ed Bingo Checking Charts (see SE-65)
Shoe box or small box
Pencils (mark the card while playing and discard the card when through)
Note: Laminate the cards for a more permanent setup and use pennies or bingo chips to mark the cards.

Directions:
1. Pass out a Blank Bingo Card and a Bingo Checking Chart to each student. Have the students fill in their cards by choosing any five words with corresponding numbers under the *B* and placing them in the appropriate column (see Figure 1). Continue to do the same by picking any five words and numbers under I, G, and O. Choose four words and numbers under N since there is a free space.
Note: There will be little or no arguing about the "terrible" card each player received since they designed the card themselves.
2. Collect the Bingo Checking Charts.
3. Bingo is played by calling out numbers chosen at random. Photocopy two copies of the Bingo Checking Chart and laminate if possible. Cut one chart into squares and place them in the shoe box. Use the box when drawing numbers and the other chart for reference. After calling a number, place the cutout square over its corresponding square on the chart so as to keep track of the numbers drawn.
4. Play by regular Bingo rules; that is, pick a square and call out the number and word ("O-74: Chlamydia"). Wait a few moments for students to search and then continue. Call out numbers and words until someone shouts, "BINGO!"
5. Decide ahead of time the form of Bingo to be played. Some examples:
    a. vertical, horizontal, or diagonal rows
    b. X
    c. four corners
    d. H or T
    e. outside edges
    f. entire card
6. When a student yells, "Bingo," check your chart and award that person or team a point.

BLANK BINGO CARD (SE-64)

B	I	N	G	O
		Free Space		

SAMPLE BINGO CARD

B	I	N	G	O
B7 Egg Cell	I19 Foreskin	N40 Placenta	G50 Sponge	O68 Herpes Simplex II
B6 Progesterone	I17 Penis	N43 Embryo	G46 Pills	O71 Tricho- moniasis
B1 Uterus	I30 Erection	**Free Space**	G56 Cervical Cap	O63 Scabies
B12 Menstruation	I21 Urethra	N38 Crowning	G57 IUD	O64 Vaginitis
B15 Womb	I28 Prostate	N45 Breech Birth	G60 Abstinence	O74 Chlamydia

Figure 1. Sample Bingo Card

SEX EDUCATION BINGO CHECKING CHART (SE-65)

B	B1 Uterus	B2 Vagina	B3 Ovulation	B4 Labia	B5 Breasts	B6 Progesterone	B7 Egg Cell
B8 Fallopian Tubes	B9 Ovaries	B10 Clitoris	B11 Hymen	B12 Menstruation	B13 Cervix	B14 Estrogen	B15 Womb
I	I16 Testes	I17 Penis	I18 Circumcision	I19 Foreskin	I20 Seminal Vesicle	I21 Urethra	I22 Cowper's Glands
I23 Seminiferous Tubules	I24 Semen	I25 Vas Deferens	I26 Scrotum	I27 Epididymis	I28 Prostate	I29 Ejaculation	I30 Erection
N	N31 Pregnancy	N32 Trimester	N33 Gynecologist	N34 Umbilical Cord	N35 Fetus	N36 Labor	N37 Episiotomy
N38 Crowning	N39 Caesarean Section	N40 Placenta	N41 Amniotic Sac	N42 Obstetrician	N43 Embryo	N44 Contraction	N45 Breech Birth
G	G46 Pills	G47 Spermicidal Foam	G48 Diaphragm	G49 Condom	G50 Sponge	G51 Tubal Ligation	G52 Vasectomy
G53 Douche	G54 Nonoxynol-9	G55 Spermicidal Jelly	G56 Cervical Cap	G57 Intra-uterine Device	G58 Rhythm	G59 Withdrawal	G60 Abstinence
O	O61 AIDS	O62 Nongonococcal Urethritis	O63 Scabies	O64 Vaginitis	O65 Antibiotics	O66 Penicillin	O67 STD
O68 Herpes Simplex II	O69 Pelvic Inflammatory Disease	O70 Genital Warts	O71 Trichomoniasis	O72 Syphilis	O73 Gonorrhea	O74 Chlamydia	O75 Pubic Lice

ACTIVITY 12: WHAT WAS THE QUESTION?

Concept/
Description: The idea behind this game is to listen to the answers and try to come up with the questions. Use it as a test review or to reinforce knowledge of the material covered.

Objective: To score the most points by successfully stating questions to fit the given answers.

Materials: Question and Answer Key (see SE-66)
Chalkboard, chalk, and eraser

Directions:
1. Draw the categories and point values on the board as shown in Figure 2.

2. Divide the class into two teams and appoint a spokesperson for each group. The spokesperson will confer with his or her team and give the "answer" in question form. Allow 15 seconds to confer and answer.

3. Play proceeds as follows: Team A chooses a category and a point value (the higher the point value, the more difficult the question). For example, Team A might choose "STDs for 20." From the Question and Answer Key the teacher would read, "What PID stands for." The team confers and the spokesperson says, "What is Pelvic Inflammatory Disease?" The teacher informs them that they are correct and awards Team A 20 points. That category is then erased from the board. It is now Team B's turn.

4. If Team B is incorrect, the point total is deducted from B's score even if the total score goes into negative numbers, and the category remains open.

5. Play continues and Team A may choose the question Team B answered incorrectly, or a new category. To keep both teams involved, always alternate play from team to team regardless of correct or incorrect answers.

6. Continue play until all the categories are used.
   Note: Make several copies of the Question and Answer Key and cross off categories on your sheet, as well as on the board to avoid discrepancies.

MALE	FEMALE	BIRTH	STD'S	CONTRA.
10	10	10	10	10
20	20	20	20	20
30	30	30	30	30
40	40	40	40	40
50	50	50	50	50

Figure 2. Chalkboard setup for the game.

QUESTION AND ANSWER KEY (SE-66)

	MALE	FEMALE	CHILDBIRTH	STD's	CONTRACEPTION
10 points ?	What is the penis?	What is the vagina?	What is an obstetrician?	What is sexually transmitted disease?	What is a condom?
A.	The male organ of intercourse.	The female organ of intercourse.	A doctor who delivers babies.	What STD stands for.	A rubber sheath over the penis.
20 points ?	What is the scrotum?	What are the ovaries?	What are signs of labor?	What is pelvic inflammatory disease?	What is withdrawal?
A.	The sac that regulates the temperature of the testes.	The organs that produce eggs.	Contractions, the "show," water breaks.	What PID stands for.	Ejaculation occurs outside the vagina.
30 points ?	What is testosterone?	What is estrogen?	What is a breech birth?	What is pubic lice?	What is a diaphragm?
A.	The male hormone responsible for changes during puberty.	The female hormone responsible for changes during puberty.	A baby born feet or buttocks first.	Intense itching and nits on the pubic hair.	A rubber sperm barrier inside the vagina.
40 points ?	What is the prostate?	What is the cervix?	What is the placenta?	What are genital warts?	What is rhythm?
A.	The most common site of cancer in men.	The most common site of cancer in women.	The organ that nourishes the fetus.	Pink or reddish warts on the genitals.	Abstinence during ovulation.
50 points ?	What is a vasectomy?	What is tubal ligation?	What is the umbilical cord?	What is syphilis?	What is the pill?
A.	The vas deferens are cut and tied.	The Fallopian tubes are cut and tied.	The connection from the baby's navel to the placenta.	Disease characterized by chancres.	A chemical that prevents ovulation.

ACTIVITY 13: SLAM DUNK!!
(Trash Can Basketball)

Concept/ Description: Students can earn "shots" at the basket by correctly answering questions relating to sex education.

Objective: To score the most points by correctly answering questions and making "baskets."

Materials: Slam Dunk Questions Sheet (SE-67)
Chalkboard
Chalk and eraser
Trash can or container
Three small foam balls or paper wads

Directions:

1. Set the trash can about 10 to 15 feet from the balls or paper wads.

2. Divide the class into two teams.

3. Ask one member of Team A a question from the question sheet. (Rotate who answers so that all team members get a turn.)

4. If the answer is correct, Team A gets one point, plus the person who answered gets one shot at the basket. If the shot goes in, the team gets an additional point.
   Note: If the team answers correctly, but misses the shot, it still receives the point for answering correctly. If a team does not answer correctly, a shot is not attempted.

5. Play then proceeds to Team B.

6. Continue until time is up. The team with the most points is the winner.

Variations:

1. Use questions with one-, two-, or three-part answers. If answered correctly, the team receives one point plus one, two, or three shots.

2. A team member must shoot a basket before the team can answer a question.

SLAM DUNK QUESTIONS (SE-67)

1. What is another name for the birth canal? (vagina)

2. Name the process by which the uterus sheds its lining. (menstruation)

3. Where is sperm produced? (testes)

4. Name the organs that produce egg cells. (ovaries)

5. Name the organ that protects and regulates the temperature of the testes. (scrotum)

6. Where is sperm stored? (epididymis)

7. Name the tube that is severed during a vasectomy. (vas deferens)

8. Name the tube that carries a mature egg from the ovary to the uterus. (Fallopian tube)

9. What type of doctor specializes in the female reproductive system? (gynecologist)

10. In what organ is the baby housed during pregnancy? (uterus)

11. Name the tube that carries both urine and semen out of the body in males and only urine in females. (urethra)

12. Name the hormone responsible for masculine changes during puberty. (testosterone)

13. Name the organ that nourishes the baby in the uterus. (placenta)

14. Name the sac of water that protects and cushions the baby during pregnancy. (amniotic sac)

15. Name the sheath of skin at the entrance of the vagina. (hymen)

16. What is the operation to remove the foreskin of the penis called? (circumcision)

17. Name the method of birth control in which the penis is removed from the vagina just before ejaculation. (withdrawal)

18. What is the safest and most effective method of birth control? (abstinence)

19. What substance can a condom be treated with to help prevent the spread of STDs? (nonoxynol-9)

20. Name the most common site of cancer in women. (cervix)

21. Name the most common site of cancer in men. (prostate)

22. What signals the onset of puberty in males? (first ejaculation of semen)

23. What signals the onset of puberty in females? (menstruation)

24. When a woman's water breaks it is a sign of what? (labor)

25. Name a female hormone other than estrogen. (progesterone)

ANSWER KEYS
TO
REPRODUCIBLES

PUBERTY IN FEMALES (SE-1)

UNDERARM HAIR

BREASTS DEVELOP

WAISTLINE SLIMS

HIPS BROADEN

OVULATION

PUBIC HAIR

MENSTRUATION

Understanding puberty worksheet

PUBERTY IN MALES (SE-2)

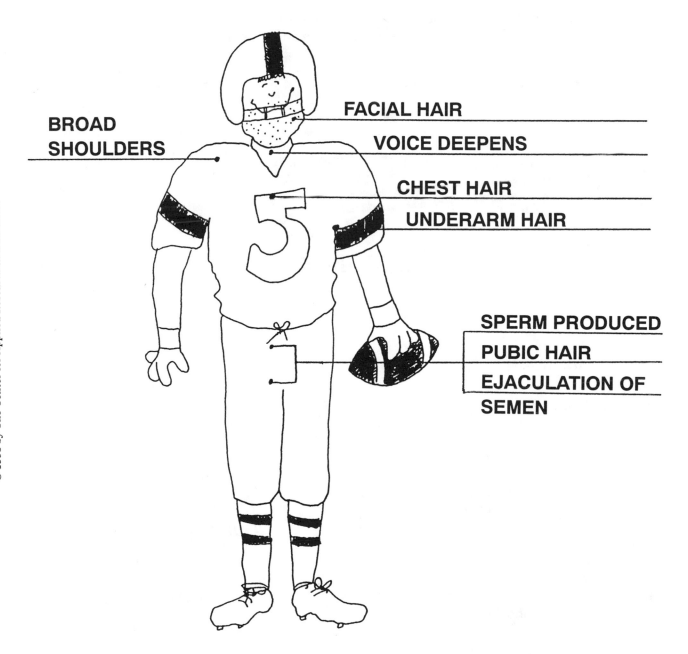

BROAD SHOULDERS

FACIAL HAIR

VOICE DEEPENS

CHEST HAIR

UNDERARM HAIR

SPERM PRODUCED

PUBIC HAIR

EJACULATION OF SEMEN

Understanding puberty worksheet

ENDOCRINE FUNCTIONS (SE-3)

DIRECTIONS: Label the parts of the Endocrine System and match each gland to its function by placing the correct letter in the blank.

__C__ 1. thyroid gland

__F__ 2. pineal gland

__H__ 3. adrenal glands

__D__ 4. pituitary gland

__A__ 5. pancreas

__I__ 6. ovaries

__G__ 7. testes

__E__ 8. parathyroids

__B__ 9. thymus gland

a. secretes a digestive juice and produces insulin
b. located near the heart and may play an important role in the immune system
c. produces thyroxine
d. master gland that has many regulatory functions
e. four small glands that regulate calcium and phosphorus
f. located in the brain and may have to do with sexual development
g. produces testosterone and sperm cells
h. located at the top of each kidney and secretes steroid hormones
i. produces egg cells, estrogen, and progesterone

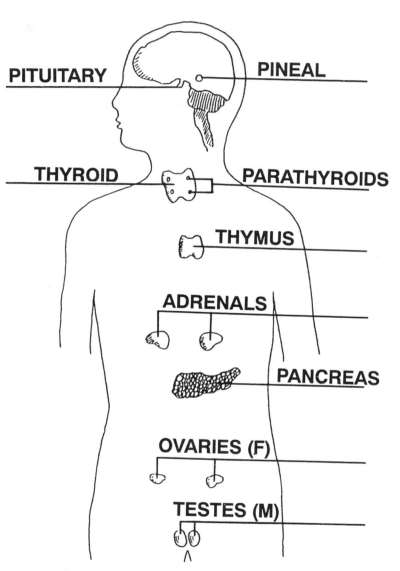

PITUITARY

PINEAL

THYROID

PARATHYROIDS

THYMUS

ADRENALS

PANCREAS

OVARIES (F)

TESTES (M)

UNDERSTANDING HORMONES (SE-4)

DIRECTIONS: Next to each endocrine gland listed is a list of the hormones that the gland secretes. Find what job or function each hormone performs and describe what occurs when the gland is overactive or underactive.

GLAND	HORMONE	FUNCTION	OVER	UNDER
pituitary	somatropic	growth — muscles, kidneys, fat tissue, liver, bones, height	gigantism acromegaly	midget dwarf
	TSH	regulates the size and activity of the thyroid gland		
	ACTH	triggers the adrenal glands		
	FSH	development of the cells surrounding the egg cell		
	LH	ovulation - tells ovaries and testes to produce hormones		
	antidiuretic	regulates the body's water balance		
	oxytocin	stimulates the smooth muscle in the internal organs		
thyroid	thyroxine	iodine—causes chemical reaction, affects all tissues	energy increase— overactive	sluggishness, tiredness
adrenals	steroids	group of chemical compounds that affect many functions		
	aldosterone	maintains body's water balance		
	cortisone	controls metabolism, helps to cope with stress		
	adrenaline	"emergency hormone" increases heart rate, breathing, etc.		
pancreas	glucagon	causes liver to convert glycogen to glucose		
	insulin	regulates the blood-sugar level		diabetes mellitus
ovaries	estrogen	development of secondary sex characteristics		
	progesterone	development of secondary sex characteristics		
testes	testosterone	development of secondary sex characteristics		

ENDOCRINE MATCH-UP (SE-5)

DIRECTIONS: Match the endocrine gland with the letter of the hormone or condition associated with it. There may be more than one letter for each gland.

GLAND	HORMONE/FUNCTION/DISORDER
B, F, I, K, O 1. pituitary	a. progesterone
L, P 2. thyroid	b. somatotropic hormone
C, D, M 3. adrenals	c. adrenaline
H 4. pancreas	d. cortisone
A, G, J 5. ovaries	e. sperm cells
E, N 6. testes	f. FSH
	g. egg cells
	h. insulin
	i. dwarfism
	j. estrogen
	k. acromegaly
	l. thyroxine
	m. steroids
	n. testosterone
	o. TSH
	p. goiter

FEMALE REPRODUCTIVE SYSTEM DIAGRAM (SE-6)

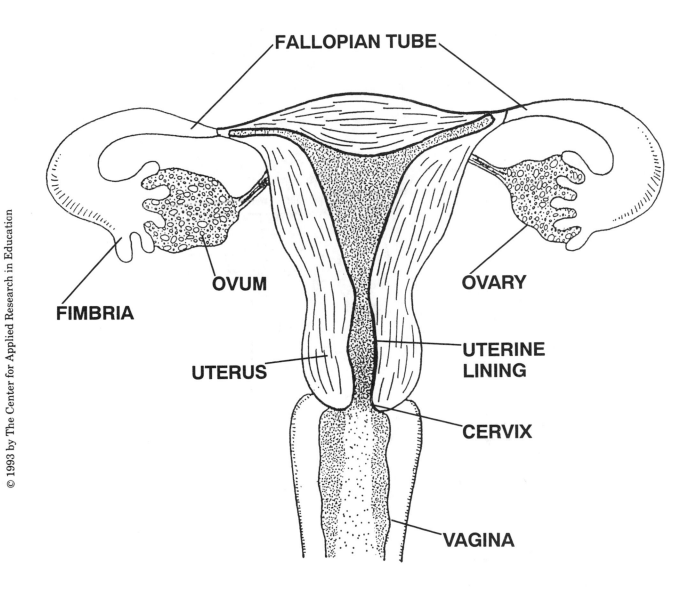

FALLOPIAN TUBE

OVUM

OVARY

FIMBRIA

UTERINE
LINING

UTERUS

CERVIX

VAGINA

DIRECTIONS: Using the words below, label the parts of the female reproductive system:

CERVIX	UTERUS	OVUM	FALLOPIAN TUBE
FIMBRIA	OVARY	VAGINA	UTERINE LINING

FEMALE REPRODUCTIVE SYSTEM (SE-7)
External View

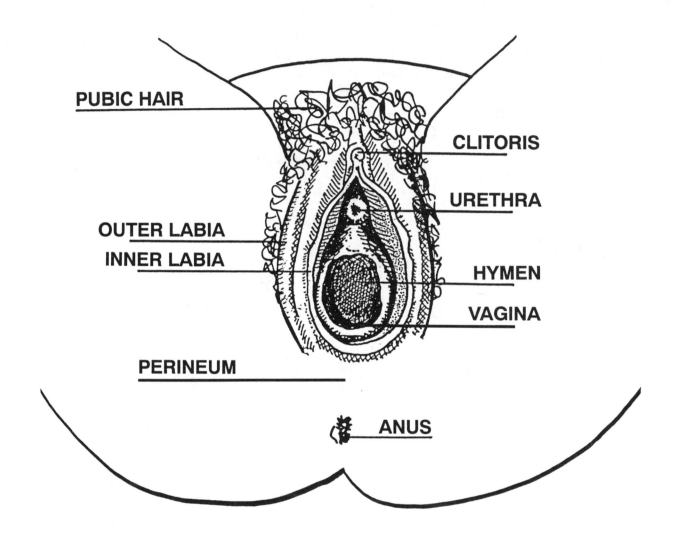

PUBIC HAIR

CLITORIS

URETHRA

OUTER LABIA

INNER LABIA

HYMEN

VAGINA

PERINEUM

ANUS

DIRECTIONS: Label the diagram using the words below:

PUBIC HAIR	CLITORIS	VAGINA
INNER LABIA	OUTER LABIA	ANUS
URETHRA	HYMEN	PERINEUM

THE MENSTRUAL CYCLE (SE-8)

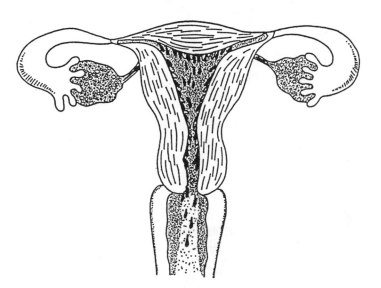

DURING MENSTRUATION

Days 1-5:

Menstruation occurs and the lining of the uterus, with a small amount of blood, leaves the body. At this time another egg is maturing in the ovary.

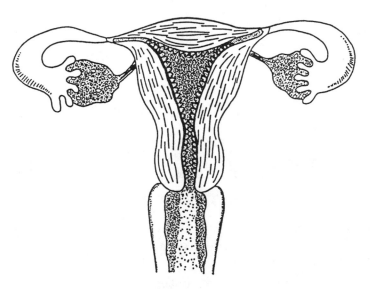

AFTER MENSTRUATION:

Days 6-15:

The lining of the uterus repairs itself and once again prepares for a fertilized egg. Around days 13 to 15 an egg is released from an ovary. This is called OVULATION.

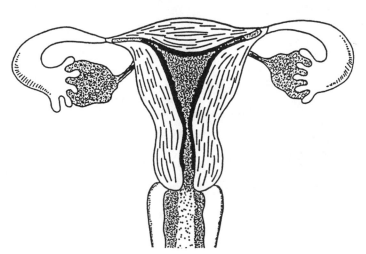

BEFORE MENSTRUATION:

Days 16-28:

If the egg is fertilized by the male sperm cell, it embeds itself in the wall of the uterus. If the egg is not fertilized, the blood vessels in the wall of the uterus shrink and break down. Then menstruation begins again.

THE FEMALE REPRODUCTIVE SYSTEM (SE-9)

DIRECTIONS: Using the sixteen words provided, fill in the blanks to make this explanation of the female reproductive system correct. Each word will be used only once.

cervix	ovaries
clitoris	ovulation
egg cells	ovum
estrogen	progesterone
Fallopian tubes	puberty
hymen	sperm cell
labia	uterus
menstruation	vagina

First, __EGG__ __CELLS__ are produced in two almond-shaped organs known as the __OVARIES__. During the process of __OVULATION__, a mature egg (__OVUM__) is released and enters one of two __FALLOPIAN__ __TUBES__. For a few days the egg cell travels towards the pear-shaped __UTERUS__. The lining of this organ thickens in preparation for a fertilized egg. If the egg is not fertilized by the male __SPERM__ __CELL__, it will leave the body together with the lining of the uterus and a small amount of blood. This is called __MENSTRUATION__.

The lower portion of the uterus is called the __CERVIX__ and is a common site of cancer in women. The female organ of intercourse is the __VAGINA__. A circular fold of skin is usually present at the entrance to this organ and is called the __HYMEN__. Outside of this organ are folds of skin covered with pubic hair known as the __LABIA__. Between these skin folds is a small, round, sensitive area of skin called the __CLITORIS__.

The development of the reproductive system is triggered by the hormones __ESTROGEN__ and __PROGESTERONE__, which cause many physical changes in a girl. This period of change is called __PUBERTY__.

MALE REPRODUCTIVE SYSTEM DIAGRAM (SE-10)

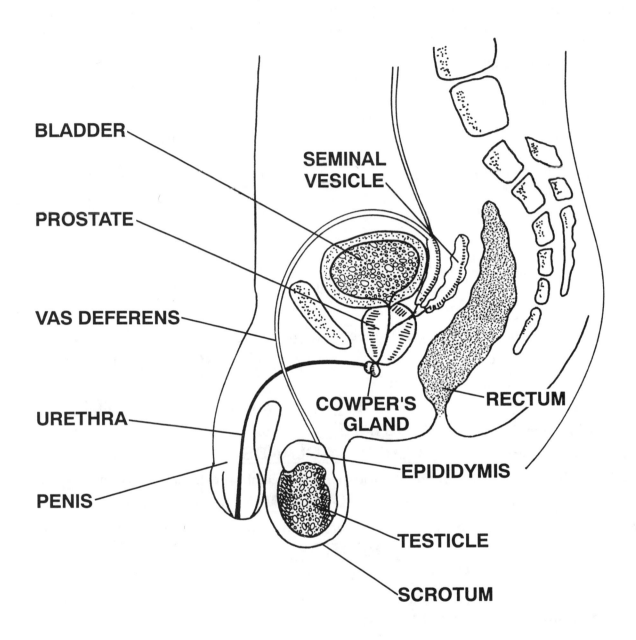

BLADDER

SEMINAL VESICLE

PROSTATE

VAS DEFERENS

URETHRA

PENIS

COWPER'S GLAND

RECTUM

EPIDIDYMIS

TESTICLE

SCROTUM

DIRECTIONS: Using the words below, label the parts of the male reproductive system:

PENIS	RECTUM	BLADDER	TESTICLE
URETHRA	EPIDIDYMIS	PROSTATE	COWPER'S GLAND
SCROTUM	VAS DEFERENS	SEMINAL VESICLE	

THE MALE REPRODUCTIVE SYSTEM (SE-11)

DIRECTIONS: Using the fifteen words provided, fill in the blanks to make this explanation of the male reproductive system correct. Each will be used only once.

Cowper's glands
epididymis
erection
nocturnal emissions
orgasm
penis
prostate
scrotum

semen
seminal vesicle
sperm
testes
urine
urethra
vas deferens

First, __**SPERM**__ are produced in the small seminiferous tubules of the __**TESTES**__. These oval-shaped glands are protected by a sac called the __**SCROTUM**__. After the sperm cells are produced, they are stored in a large coiled tube on the outer surface of each testicle called the __**EPIDIDYMIS**__. From this tube the sperm go into a larger tube called the __**VAS**__ __**DEFERENS**__, which eventually carries them to the external male reproductive organ, the __**PENIS**__. Along the way sperm is nourished by a sugary fluid from the __**SEMINAL**__ __**VESICLE**__, a chemical fluid from the __**PROSTATE**__ which is the most common site of cancer in men, and fluid from the __**COWPER'S**__ __**GLANDS**__ which are two small glands located near the bladder. These fluids plus the sperm cells combine to form __**SEMEN**__, the fluid ejaculated from the penis during __**ORGASM**__. Before a male can ejaculate, the spongy tissue surrounding the penis becomes engorged with blood causing the penis to become stiff and hard. This is known as an __**ERECTION**__. The tube that carries the semen from the body is the __**URETHRA**__. This tube also carries __**URINE**__ from the bladder. Males can also have uncontrolled ejaculation during sleep, which are called __**NOCTURNAL**__ __**EMISSIONS**__.

WHO'S WHO VOCABULARY WORKSHEET (SE-12)

DIRECTIONS: Read each word below and place an F if it is part of the female reproductive system, an M if it is part of the male reproductive system, and a B if it is part of both systems.

B	1. testosterone	**F**	16. Fallopian tubes
F	2. labia	**M**	17. nocturnal emission
M	3. sperm	**F**	18. estrogen
B	4. genitals	**M**	19. scrotum
B	5. pubic hair	**F**	20. ovulation
B	6. puberty	**M**	21. semen
M	7. ejaculation	**M**	22. erection
B	8. hormones	**F**	23. progesterone
F	9. ovaries	**B**	24. urethra
F	10. cervix	**F**	25. placenta
F	11. menstruation	**M**	26. foreskin
M	12. testes	**F**	27. hymen
F	13. vagina	**M**	28. prostate
B	14. bladder	**F**	29. clitoris
F	15. uterus	**M**	30. seminal vesicles

Do I have that estrogen stuff or do you?

ANATOMY CHALLENGE (SE-13)

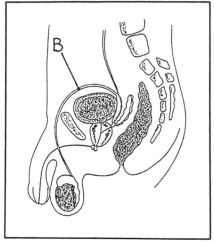
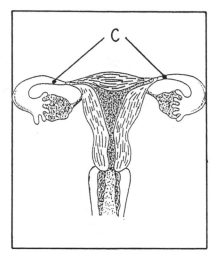
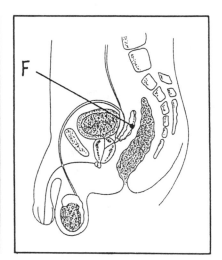
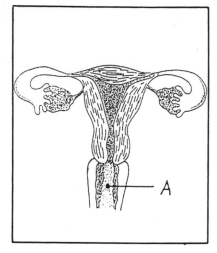
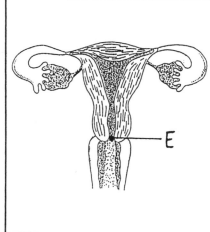
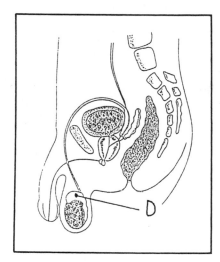

DIRECTIONS: Label each part of the reproductive system as it corresponds to the letter.

A. **VAGINA** _____ D. **EPIDIDYMIS** _____

B. **VAS DEFERENS** _____ E. **CERVIX** _____

C. **FALLOPIAN TUBES** _____ F. **SEMINAL VESICLE** _____

VOCABULARY CHALLENGE (SE-14)

DIRECTIONS: Place the correct letter in the blank to the left. Letters may be used only once.

U	1. testosterone	A. brings urine and semen out of body through the penis
W	2. fetus	B. adds a chemical fluid to the semen
S	3. semen	C. when the penis becomes engorged with blood and hard
Y	4. fertilization	D. where fertilization takes place
C	5. erection	E. glands that produce the egg cells and hormones
B	6. prostate gland	F. first two months of development in the uterus
E	7. ovaries	G. organ that nourishes the fetus
O	8. egg cells	H. stores sperm cells
Q	9. cervix	I. female organ of intercourse; birth canal
L	10. seminal vesicles	J. female erectile tissue between the labia
T	11. testes	K. houses the fetus during pregnancy
X	12. vas deferens	L. adds a sugary fluid to semen
R	13. ejaculation	M. folds of skin outside of the vagina
V	14. puberty	N. a hormone produced in the ovaries
Z	15. scrotum	O. cells produced in the ovaries
I	16. vagina	P. cells produced in the testes
D	17. Fallopian tubes	Q. entrance to the uterus
F	18. embryo	R. when the semen leaves the penis
N	19. estrogen	S. fluid ejaculated from the penis
K	20. uterus	T. organ that produces sperm
M	21. labia	U. male hormone
H	22. epididymis	V. begins at about age 12 or 13
A	23. urethra	W. last 7 months of prenatal development
J	24. clitoris	X. tube that carries sperm from testes
P	25. sperm cells	Y. sperm cell joins egg cell
G	26. placenta	Z. sac that regulates the temperature of the testes

YOU'RE OUTTA HERE (SE-15)

DIRECTIONS: In each group, one item does not belong. Circle the item that does not belong and briefly explain why.

1.   ESTROGEN   PROGESTERONE   (TESTOSTERONE)

Why? __**NOT A FEMALE HORMONE**_____

2.   (AMOEBA)   EMBRYO   FETUS

Why? __**NOT A STAGE OF DEVELOPMENT IN THE WOMB**____

3.   (THYMUS)   AMNIOTIC SAC   PLACENTA

Why? __**NOT PART OF THE UTERUS DURING PREGNANCY**___

4.   FALLOPIAN TUBE   VAGINA   (PROSTATE)

Why? __**NOT PART OF THE FEMALE REPRODUCTIVE SYSTEM**__

5.   SEMINAL VESICLE   VAS DEFERENS   (OVARIES)

Why? __**NOT PART OF THE MALE REPRODUCTIVE SYSTEM**__

6.   URETHRA   BLADDER   (TESTES)

Why? __**NOT PRESENT IN BOTH THE MALE AND FEMALE**___

7.   (CONDOM)   TUBAL LIGATION   VASECTOMY

Why? __**NOT A PERMANENT METHOD OF CONTRACEPTION**__

8.   (TUBERCULOSIS)   CHLAMYDIA   TRICHOMONIASIS

Why? __**NOT AN STD**_____

9.   1ST EJACULATION   (MENOPAUSE)   ONSET OF MENSTRUATION

Why? __**NOT A SIGN OF PUBERTY**_____

10.   CERVIX   (URETHRA)   PROSTATE

Why? __**NOT A COMMON SITE OF CANCER**_____

REPRODUCTIVE SYSTEM: DISEASES & DISORDERS (SE-16)

DIRECTIONS: Choose the best answer by circling the correct letter.

1. A tear in the abdominal wall near the scrotum which may allow the intestines to push through is a(n):
   a. appendicitis
   B. INGUINAL HERNIA
   c. form of prostate cancer

2. The inability to reproduce because the sperm cells are unable to fertilize the egg is called:
   A. STERILITY
   b. impotence
   c. premature ejaculation

3. An abnormal growth of cells is called:
   a. mono
   b. hepatitis
   C. CANCER

4. A common site of cancer in men is the:
   a. epididymis
   B. PROSTATE
   c. Cowper's gland

5. A sign of testicular cancer is:
   A. NODULES ON THE TESTES
   b. nausea
   c. a severe skin rash

6. A condition in which the inner lining of the uterus is present abnormally in the abdominal cavity is called:
   a. psychosis
   B. ENDOMETRIOSIS
   c. scoliosis

7. Which is NOT a type of vaginitis?
   a. trichomoniasis
   b. yeast infection
   C. PMS

8. For which reason is a Pap smear given?
   a. to detect AIDS
   B. TO DETECT CERVICAL CANCER
   c. to detect breast cancer

9. Which is NOT a cause of sterility?
   a. an untreated STD
   b. certain illnesses, such as mumps in an adult
   C. DEPRESSION

10. Depression, mood swings, bloating, anxiety, and irritability are symptoms of:
    A. PMS
    b. breast cancer
    c. vaginitis

SIGNS OF PREGNANCY (SE-17)

DIRECTIONS: Choose the best answer from the list below and fill in the blanks. The answers will be used only once.

SIGNS OF PREGNANCY

1. Period is _____ **LATE** _____ or missed.

2. Abnormal period, lighter or _____ **SHORTER** _____ than usual.

3. Breast _____ **TENDERNESS** _____ or fullness.

4. Nausea and sometimes _____ **VOMITING** _____.

5. Changes in _____ **APPETITE** _____.

6. Frequent _____ **URINATION** _____.

7. Fatigue or _____ **TIREDNESS** _____.

PREGNANCY TESTS

1. URINE TEST—to detect the presence of _____ **HCG** _____, a hormone that is produced when a woman is pregnant.

2. PELVIC EXAM—to check the _____ **SIZE** _____ of the uterus.

3. BLOOD TEST—rarely used because _____ **URINE** _____ tests are simpler to use and just as accurate.

HCG	TENDERNESS	LATE	URINATION	APPETITE
SHORTER	VOMITING	SIZE	TIREDNESS	URINE

110

© 1993 by The Center for Applied Research in Education

DEVELOPMENT OF THE EMBRYO AND FETUS (SE-18)

3-4 WEEKS

Called an EMBRYO
Heartbeat
Brain forming
1/4 inch long
Lungs forming

6 WEEKS

Fingers, toes
Ears
Skin forming

8 WEEKS

1-1/2 inches long
1/30 of an ounce
All organs have
   begun to develop

12 WEEKS

Now called a FETUS
Movement felt
3 inches long
Can swallow

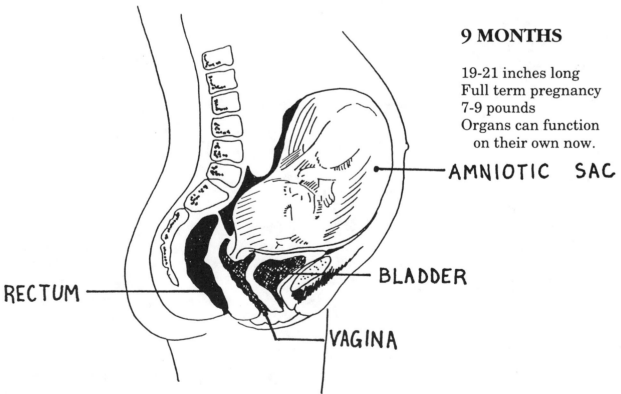

9 MONTHS

19-21 inches long
Full term pregnancy
7-9 pounds
Organs can function
   on their own now.

AMNIOTIC SAC

BLADDER

RECTUM

VAGINA

PREGNANCY AND CHILDBIRTH STAGES (SE-19)

DIRECTIONS: Number the stages of pregnancy and childbirth in the correct order.

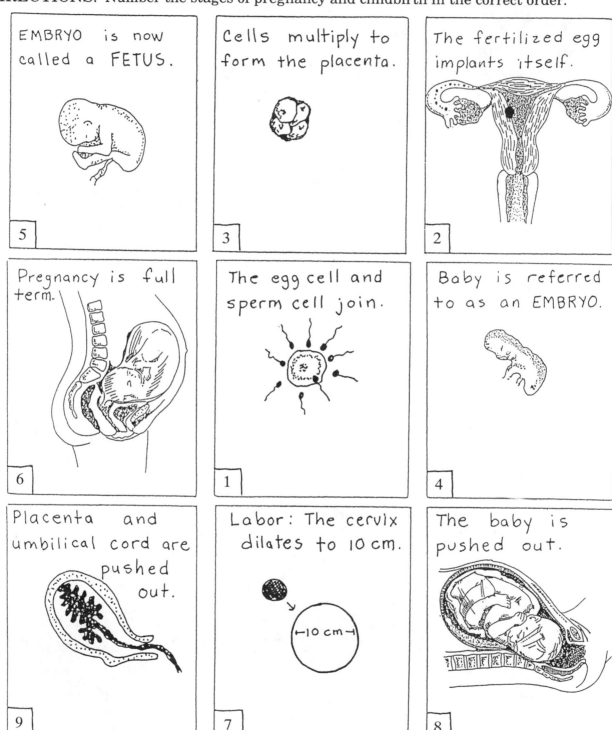

EMBRYO is now called a FETUS.

5

Cells multiply to form the placenta.

3

The fertilized egg implants itself.

2

Pregnancy is full term.

6

The egg cell and sperm cell join.

1

Baby is referred to as an EMBRYO.

4

Placenta and umbilical cord are pushed out.

9

Labor: The cervix dilates to 10 cm.

7

The baby is pushed out.

8

CHILDBIRTH CROSSWORD CHALLENGE (SE-20)

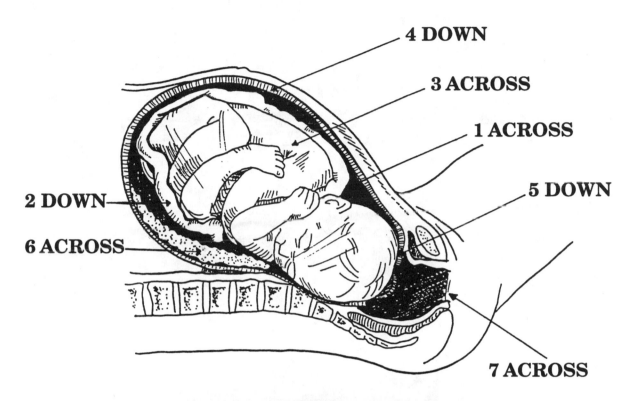

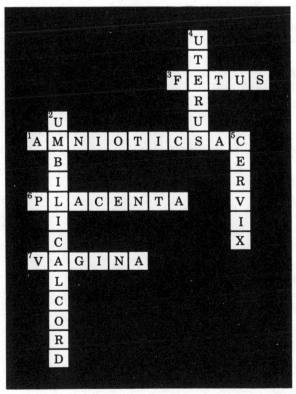

CONTRACEPTIVE MATCH-UP (SE-21)

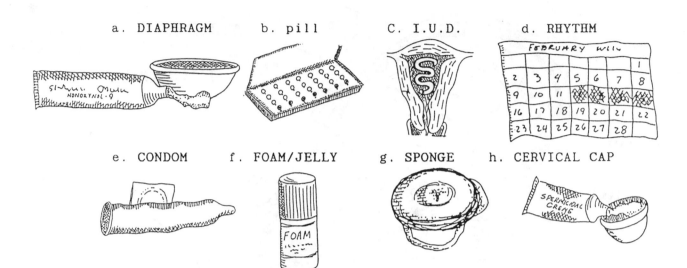

a. DIAPHRAGM   b. pill   C. I.U.D.   d. RHYTHM

e. CONDOM   f. FOAM/JELLY   g. SPONGE   h. CERVICAL CAP

DIRECTIONS: Match the picture with the correct statement by placing the letters in the blank to the left of each statement. Letters may be used more than once.

E _____ 1. Rubber sheath placed over the penis.

D _____ 2. Abstinence during ovulation.

A _____ 3. Used with jelly to block the sperm from entering the uterus.

B _____ 4. Prevents ovulation.

E, G _____ 5. An over-the-counter sperm barrier that is used with spermicide.

E _____ 6. If treated with nonoxynol 9, this method also helps prevent the spread of STDs.

C _____ 7. Inserted into the uterus by a physician.

B _____ 8. May cause initial weight gain and is dangerous to women over 35 who smoke.

H _____ 9. Blocks the entrance to the uterus by fitting directly over the cervix.

C _____ 10. A method of birth control considered unsafe for young girls and many women.

114

CHEMICAL METHODS OF CONTRACEPTION (SE-22)

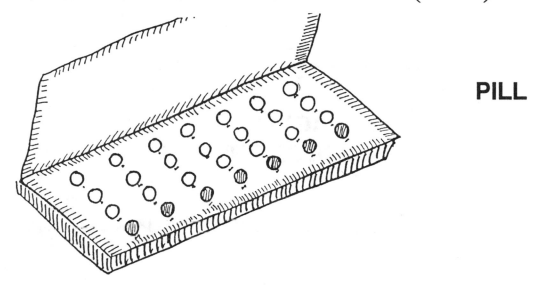

PILL

Description: **A PILL COMPOSED OF SYNTHETIC HORMONES THAT STOPS THE OVARY FROM RELEASING AN EGG.**

Effectiveness %: **>99%**

How do you obtain this? **SEE A GYNECOLOGIST OR FAMILY PLANNING CLINIC. MUST HAVE A PRESCRIPTION.**

Possible side effects: **NAUSEA, BREAST TENDERNESS, WEIGHT GAIN; DANGEROUS TO USE IF OVER 35 AND A SMOKER.**

Other: **DO NOT USE SOMEONE ELSE'S PILLS. NORMAL MENSTRUAL CYCLES STILL OCCUR. HELPS TO REGULATE PERIODS AND CAN REDUCE SOME PMS SYMPTOMS. MUST BE TAKEN EVERY DAY.**

CHEMICAL METHODS OF CONTRACEPTION (SE-23)

VAGINAL SUPPOSITORIES

Description: __A SPERMICIDE IN SOLID FORM THAT MELTS AT__ __BODY TEMPERATURE. IT IS INSERTED DEEP INTO THE VAGINA.__

Effectiveness %: __78%__

How do you obtain this? __DRUG STORE, SUPERMARKET,__ __AVAILABLE OVER-THE-COUNTER.__

Possible side effects: __MAY CAUSE IRRITATION.__

Other: __MUST BE USED EVERY TIME INTERCOURSE OCCURS.__ __MAY PROVIDE SOME PROTECTION AGAINST STDS.__

CHEMICAL METHODS OF CONTRACEPTION (SE-24)

SPERMICIDAL FOAMS, JELLIES, CREAMS

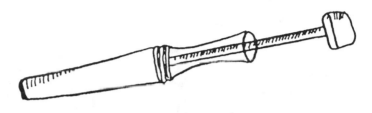

Description: **THESE ACT AS A PHYSICAL BARRIER AND CONTAIN A SPERM-KILLING CHEMICAL.**

Effectiveness %: **78%**

How do you obtain this? **DRUG STORE, SUPERMARKET, OVER-THE-COUNTER.**

Possible side effects: **MAY CAUSE IRRITATION.**

Other: **MUST BE INSERTED DEEP IN THE VAGINA AND MUST BE USED EVERY TIME INTERCOURSE OCCURS. MAY PROVIDE SOME PROTECTION AGAINST STDS.**

CHEMICAL METHODS OF CONTRACEPTION (SE-25)

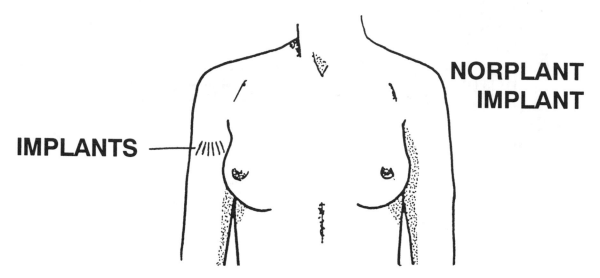

IMPLANTS

NORPLANT IMPLANT

Description: __SIX TINY HORMONE-FILLED RODS ARE PLACED UNDER__ THE SKIN OF THE UPPER ARM. THE HORMONES KEEP THE BODY FROM RELEASING AN EGG, KEEP THE LINING OF THE UTERUS FROM THICKENING, AND CAUSE CERVICAL MUCUS TO THICKEN, BLOCKING SPERM.

Effectiveness %: __>99%__

How do you obtain this? __SEE A GYNECOLOGIST OR FAMILY__ PLANNING CLINIC. 15-20 MINUTES OF MINOR SURGERY.

Possible side effects: __IRREGULAR PERIODS.__

Other: __COST IS HIGH AT FIRST, BUT IS EFFECTIVE FOR FIVE__ YEARS. ONCE REMOVED, FERTILITY IS RESTORED.

MECHANICAL METHODS OF CONTRACEPTION (SE-26)

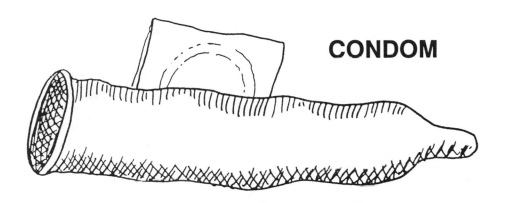

CONDOM

Description: **PLACED OVER AN ERECT PENIS. IT PREVENTS SEMEN FROM ENTERING THE VAGINA.**

Effectiveness %: **85%**

How do you obtain this? **DRUG STORE, SUPERMARKET, OVER-THE-COUNTER.**

Possible side effects: **SLIGHT POSSIBILITY OF BREAKAGE OR LEAKAGE.**

Other: **THE RIM OF THE CONDOM MUST BE HELD AFTER INTERCOURSE SO THAT THE CONDOM DOES NOT SLIP OFF AS THE PENIS IS WITHDRAWN. IF TREATED WITH NONOXYNOL-9 OFFERS SOME PROTECTION AGAINST STDS.**

MECHANICAL METHODS OF CONTRACEPTION (SE-27)

DIAPHRAGM

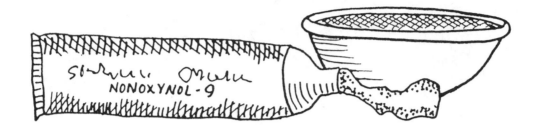

Description: ___**LARGE RUBBER CAP WHICH COVERS THE**___
CERVIX. MUST BE USED WITH SPERMICIDE.

_____

_____

Effectiveness %: ___**85%**___

How do you obtain this? ___**SEE A GYNECOLOGIST OR FAMILY**___
PLANNING CLINIC FOR FITTING AND DIRECTIONS FOR USE.

_____

Possible side effects: ___**CAN BE AWKWARD TO INSERT AND**___
REMOVE.

_____

_____

Other: ___**CAN BE INSERTED UP TO TWO HOURS BEFORE**___
INTERCOURSE, BUT MUST BE LEFT IN PLACE FOR SIX HOURS
AFTERWARDS.

_____

MECHANICAL METHODS OF CONTRACEPTION (SE-28)

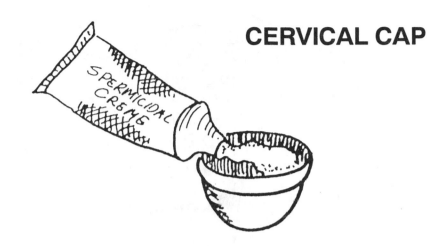

CERVICAL CAP

Description: <u>**SMALL RUBBER CAP THAT COVERS THE CERVIX.**</u>
MUST BE USED WITH SPERMICIDE.

Effectiveness %: <u>**85%**</u>

How do you obtain this? <u>**SEE A GYNECOLOGIST OR FAMILY**</u>
PLANNING CLINIC FOR FITTING AND DIRECTIONS FOR USE.

Possible side effects: <u>**CAN BE AWKWARD TO INSERT AND**</u>
REMOVE.

Other: <u>**CAN BE INSERTED UP TO TWO HOURS BEFORE**</u>
INTERCOURSE, BUT MUST BE LEFT IN PLACE FOR SIX HOURS
AFTERWARDS.

MECHANICAL METHODS OF CONTRACEPTION (SE-29)

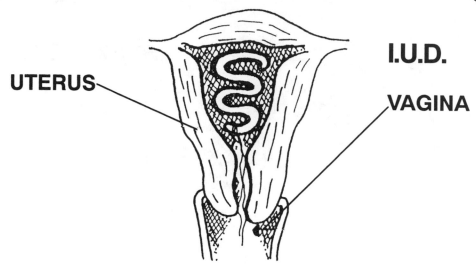

I.U.D.

UTERUS

VAGINA

Description: <u>**INTRAUTERINE DEVICE THAT IS THOUGHT TO**</u>
SOMEHOW INTERFERE WITH THE SPERM'S ABILITY TO REACH THE
EGG OR WITH A FERTILIZED EGG'S ABILITY TO IMPLANT.

Effectiveness %: <u>**97%**</u>

How do you obtain this? <u>**INSERTED BY A GYNECOLOGIST.**</u>
ONCE INSERTED MAY PREVENT PREGNANCY FOR SEVERAL YEARS.

Possible side effects: <u>**CAN CAUSE INCREASED BLEEDING**</u>
AND CRAMPS. NOT RECOMMENDED FOR WOMEN WHO HAVE NOT
HAD FAMILIES. PELVIC INFLAMMATORY DISEASE (PID).

Other: _____

MECHANICAL METHODS OF CONTRACEPTION (SE-30)

CONTRACEPTIVE SPONGE

Description: **A SPERM BARRIER TREATED WITH SPERMICIDE. THE SPONGE PHYSICALLY STOPS THE SPERM AND THE CHEMICAL KILLS THEM.**

Effectiveness %: **85%**

How do you obtain this? **DRUG STORE, SUPERMARKET, OVER-THE-COUNTER.**

Possible side effects: **THE CHEMICALS MAY CAUSE IRRITATION.**

Other: **IT CAN BE DIFFICULT TO REMOVE.**

ABSTINENCE METHODS OF CONTRACEPTION (SE-31)

ABSTINENCE

Description: **NO INTERCOURSE**

Effectiveness %: **100%**

How do you obtain this? **N/A**

Possible side effects: **N/A**

Other: **THIS IS THE ONLY 100% EFFECTIVE METHOD OF BIRTH CONTROL.**

ABSTINENCE METHODS OF CONTRACEPTION (SE-32)

WITHDRAWAL

Description: __THE PENIS IS PULLED OUT OF THE VAGINA PRIOR__
__TO EJACULATION. EJACULATION OCCURS OUTSIDE OF THE VAGINA.__

_____

Effectiveness %: __<75%_____

How do you obtain this? __N/A_____

Possible side effects: __NONE_____

_____

Other: __VERY RISKY METHOD BECAUSE IF EVEN A TINY DROP__
__OF SEMEN COMES IN CONTACT WITH VAGINAL FLUID, PREGNANCY__
__CAN OCCUR.__

ABSTINENCE METHODS OF CONTRACEPTION (SE-33)

RHYTHM

© 1993 by The Center for Applied Research in Education

Description: __INTERCOURSE IS AVOIDED DURING OVULATION.__

Effectiveness %: __<75%__

How do you obtain this? __KEEP TRACK OF MENSTRUAL CYCLE__
ON A CALENDAR OR SEE A GYNECOLOGIST OR FAMILY PLANNING CLINIC
FOR ADVICE. OBSERVATION OF BODY SIGNS, TEMPERATURE AND MUCUS.

Possible side effects: __NONE__

Other: __IT IS DIFFICULT TO DETERMINE WHEN OVULATION__
OCCURS. THEREFORE, THIS IS A RISKY METHOD OF BIRTH
CONTROL, ESPECIALLY FOR TEENAGERS.

PERMANENT METHODS OF CONTRACEPTION (SE-34)

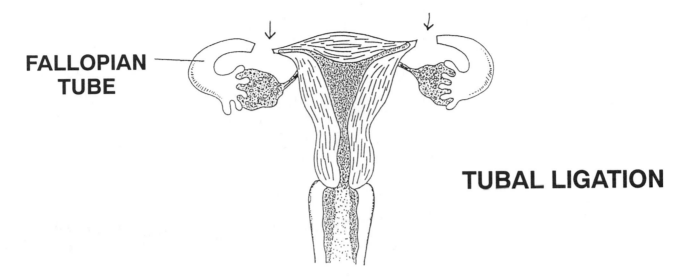

FALLOPIAN TUBE

TUBAL LIGATION

Description: **THE FALLOPIAN TUBES ARE CUT AND TIED OR CLAMPED. THE EGG CANNOT BE FERTILIZED BY THE SPERM.**

Effectiveness %: **>99%**

How do you obtain this? **SEE A GYNECOLOGIST. THIS PROCEDURE USUALLY REQUIRES GENERAL ANESTHESIA AND A BRIEF HOSPITAL STAY.**

Possible side effects: **INITIAL DISCOMFORT. PAIN IN THE SHOULDER AREA AS CO_2, USED TO MAKE VIEWING THE ORGANS EASIER, SEEPS UPWARDS. THE CO_2 WILL BE ABSORBED INTO THE BLOODSTREAM.**

Other: **OVULATION AND MENSTRUATION STILL OCCUR.**

PERMANENT METHODS OF CONTRACEPTION (SE-35)

VAS DEFERENS

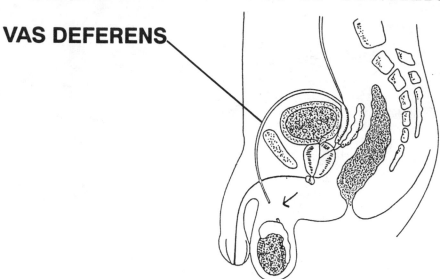

VASECTOMY

© 1993 by The Center for Applied Research in Education

Description: __THE VAS DEFERENS IS CUT AND TIED. NO SPERM__
__IS IN THE SEMEN. THE OPERATION TAKES USUALLY 15 TO 20 MIN-__
__UTES AND IS PERFORMED BY A UROLOGIST.__
_____

Effectiveness %: __>99%_____
How do you obtain this? __SEE A UROLOGIST.__
_____
_____

Possible side effects: __INITIAL DISCOMFORT AT THE SITE OF__
__THE SURGERY.__
_____
_____

Other: _____
_____
_____
_____

CONTRACEPTION COMPARISON CHART (SE-36)

METHOD	CATEGORY	HOW IT WORKS	SIDE EFFECTS	% OF EFFECTIVE-NESS	COST
Pill	Chemical	Prevents ovulation	Weight gain. Nausea. Don't use if over 35 and a smoker.	>99	$20 per month
Spermicides: foam, jelly, cream	Chemical	Spermicidal barrier	May cause irritation	78	$10 per kit
Norplant	Chemical	Rods implanted in arm. Hormone released to prevent ovulation.	Irregular bleeding	>99	$600-$800 every 5 years
Condom	Mechanical	Rubber sheath over penis. Sperm barrier.	Loss of sensation	85	50-60 cents each
Diaphragm	Mechanical	Fitted by a GYN. Sperm barrier used with jelly.	May cause irritation	85	$25 plus exam fees
IUD	Mechanical	Uncertain: May stop egg implantation.	Initial discomfort. Irregular bleeding.	97	$400 every 4 years
Sponge	Chemical and Mechanical	Sperm barrier treated with spermicide.	May cause irritation	85	$1.65 each
Total Abstinence	Abstinence	No intercourse	None	100	—
Withdrawal	Abstinence	Ejaculation occurs outside of the vagina.	None	<75	—
Rhythm	Abstinence	No sex during ovulation.	None	<75	—
Tubal Ligation	Permanent	Fallopian tubes cut and tied. Egg cannot reach uterus.	Initial discomfort	>99	$1,500-$2,000 one-time fee
Vasectomy	Permanent	Vas deferens cut and tied. No sperm in semen.	Initial discomfort	>99	$300-$500 one-time fee

STD SYMPTOMS SEEK 'N FIND (SE-37)

c	c	i	t	a	m	o	t	p	m	y	s	a	a
t	l	d	i	s	c	h	a	r	g	e	r	e	l
o	e	h	s	o	p	h	m	m	e	e	e	t	s
s	e	r	o	s	d	i	a	r	t	g	o	l	y
c	d	r	a	a	i	v	w	a	x	n	q	j	k
s	i	v	r	s	d	d	u	e	o	i	b	e	g
b	f	v	w	s	h	a	g	h	c	n	t	i	r
p	e	r	l	w	u	e	r	r	r	r	r	f	b
d	t	y	i	e	n	t	s	r	n	u	v	m	o
x	i	p	r	i	p	s	v	a	b	b	g	t	e
f	f	a	t	i	g	u	e	i	u	i	o	n	c
p	e	a	s	w	q	u	n	d	r	t	e	z	i
d	l	f	i	g	n	i	h	c	t	i	r	s
s	u	s	a	m	e	r	i	g	o	l	k	d	o

DIRECTIONS: Find ten words dealing with STD symptoms in the puzzle above. Words may be forward, backward, vertical, horizontal, or diagonal. Use the clues given to determine the words used.

CLUES:

Clue	Answer
A type of skin change.	R A S H E S
Occurs when urinating.	B U R N I N G
Pus from the penis or vagina.	D I S C H A R G E
Another type of skin change.	S O R E S
Loose, watery stools.	D I A R R H E A
Tiredness.	F A T I G U E
Having no symptoms.	A S Y M P T O M A T I C
Severe pain in this area.	P E L V I C
Occurs around genitals.	I T C H I N G
Another name for reproductive organs.	G E N I T A L S

STD FACT CHART (SE-38)

Disease	Pathogen	Where	How	Symptoms
AIDS	HIV human immuno-deficiency virus	penis, vagina, mouth, rectum, blood, mucous membranes	sex, sharing drug needles, mother to baby, transfusion	skin rashes, diarrhea, fever, weight loss, dry cough, swollen glands, loss of appetite, opportunistic infections, death
Chlamydia	chlamydia trachomatis bacteria	penis, vagina, anus, mouth	sex	painful urination, watery discharge, itching, burning of genitals, pelvic pain, bleeding between periods
Genital Herpes	herpes simplex II virus	penis, vagina, anus, mouth, transfer to eyes if sore is touched	direct, intimate contact	painful blisters or sores on the genitals, swollen glands, fever, headaches, tiredness
Syphilis	treponema pallidum bacteria	penis, vagina, anus, mouth, break in skin	congenital, mucous membrane contact w/ sores during sex	"Chancre" which goes away, fatigue, fever, sores, rash, hair loss, nervous system damage, insanity, death

DIRECTIONS: For each disease listed on the chart, fill in the *pathogen* that causes it, *where* it enters the human body, *how* it enters the human body, and the *symptoms* that are characteristic of the disease.

STD FACT CHART (SE-39)

Disease	Pathogen	Where	How	Symptoms
Gonorrhea	neisseria gonorrhea bacteria	penis vagina anus throat	direct mucous membrane contact during sex	burning discharge from penis, most women have no symptoms, can cause sterility, arthritis
Genital Warts	human papilloma virus	genitals anus	sex	warts on genitals and anus
Hepatitis	hepatitis A virus	mouth	anal-oral sex, con-taminated water	flu-like symptoms, dark urine, abdominal pain, jaundice
	hepatitis B virus	penis vagina anus mouth skin breaks blood	saliva, sex, blood, needles, etc.	
Non-Gonococ-cal Urethritis (NGU)	chlamydia ureaplasma myco-plasma trichomonas (agents)	penis vagina anus throat	direct mucous membrane contact during sex	men—watery or milky discharge from penis women—burn-ing urination

DIRECTIONS: For each disease listed on the chart, fill in the *pathogen* that causes it, *where* it enters the human body, *how* it enters the human body, and the *symptoms* that are characteristic of the disease.

STD FACT CHART (SE-40)

Disease	Pathogen	Where	How	Symptoms
Vaginitis	chlamydia gardnerella herpes candidiasis herpes trichomonas mycoplasma (agents)	vagina penis anus throat	usually sex but sometimes without sex	pain, discharge, irritation, redness, itching, odor, or asymptomatic
Pubic Lice	pediculosis pubis	pubic hair	sex bedding toilets clothing	itching, rash, pinhead-sized blood spots on underwear
Trichomoniasis	protozoan parasite	vagina	common after menstrua-tion, sex	odorous, yellow discharge, itching, burning while urinating, urethra and bladder infections
Scabies	parasitic mite that burrows under the skin	skin contact	sex, but sometimes no sex	itching in the genital area

DIRECTIONS: For each disease listed on the chart, fill in the *pathogen* that causes it, *where* it enters the human body, *how* it enters the human body, and the *symptoms* that are characteristic of the disease.

133

AIDS/STD CROSSWORD CHALLENGE (SE-43)

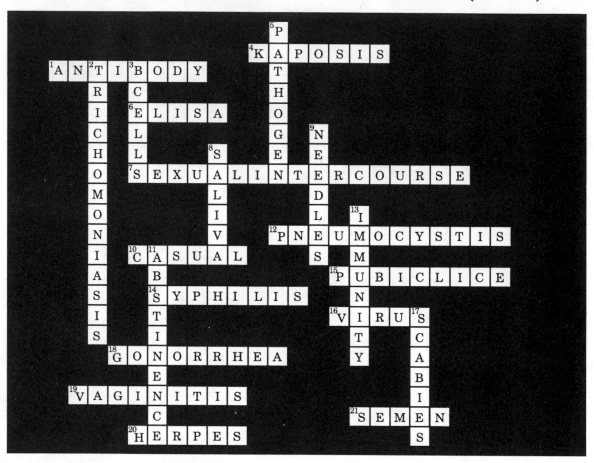

Clues

Across

1. A protein that fights off foreign substances.
4. A type of sarcoma that AIDS patients develop.
6. The first test given to determine the presence of the HIV.
7. One of the main ways STD's and AIDS is spread. (2 words)
10. AIDS is NOT spread through _____ contact, such as hugging or kissing.
12. A type of pneumonia that AIDS patients develop.
14. An STD characterized by open sores known as chancres.
15. An STD characterized by intense itching and nits attached to the pubic hair. (2 words)
16. The type of pathogen that causes AIDS.
18. An STD that is caused by bacteria that lives in the warm, moist areas of the body and is one of the most common communicable diseases.
19. A common inflammation of the vagina.
20. An incurable virus that causes blister-ing sores in the genital area.
21. The fluid ejaculated from the penis.

Down

2. A vaginal infection that is caused by a protozoan parasite.
3. The type of lymphocytes that produce antibodies. (2 words)
5. A microorganism that causes infectious diseases.
8. A body fluid that is present in the mouth and does not transmit the AIDS virus.
9. When intravenous drug users share _____ AIDS can be trans-mitted.
11. The only sure way to avoid AIDS and STD's.
13. The body's ability to fight off harmful substances.
17. A condition in which mites burrow under the skin.

WHAT IS AIDS? (SE-44)

DIRECTIONS: Fill in the missing letters to give an accurate explanation of AIDS.

The **HUMAN** immunodeficiency **VIRUS** is the pathogen that causes

AIDS. AIDS stands for acquired **IMMUNE** deficiency

SYNDROME. Though the virus is very powerful, it cannot live

OUTSIDE the human body. It does live in certain body fluids, such as

BLOOD, **SEMEN**, and **VAGINAL** secretions.

AIDS is spread through sexual **INTERCOURSE** —oral,

ANAL, or vaginal. It is also spread by using contaminated **NEEDLES**,

receiving a blood **TRANSFUSION** with contaminated blood or blood

products, or it is passed from an AIDS-infected **MOTHER** to her **CHILD**

before birth.

The best prevention against infection is **ABSTINENCE**, which is

not having sex. If a person does have sex, then the relationship should be

MONOGAMOUS, having only one partner. If a person chooses the dangerous

practice of having more than one partner, then the Surgeon General recommends the use of a

CONDOM.

There is no known **CURE** for AIDS at the present time. Any person who contracts

AIDS will die.

THE HEALTHY IMMUNE SYSTEM (SE-45)

DIRECTIONS: Fill in the blanks using the words below to explain how the healthy immune system functions.

VIRUS   BACTERIA   ILLNESS   ANTIBODIES
NORMAL   ANTIBIOTICS   MULTIPLIES   IMMUNE
T-CELLS   B-CELLS   WHITE BLOOD CELLS
CHEMICALLY   PROTOZOAN   FUNGI

---

1. A germ (**VIRUS** , **BACTERIA** ,

FUNGI , **PROTOZOAN** , etc.) invades the body and

quickly **MULTIPLIES** .

2. The healthy **IMMUNE** system fights back by sending

WHITE BLOOD CELLS to destroy the invaders.

3. First, the **T-CELLS** surround and "eat" some

of the invaders, then **CHEMICALLY** notify the

4. **B-CELLS** which, in turn, produce

5. **ANTIBODIES** which destroy the germs.

6. Germs that survive the attack can cause **ILLNESS** .

7. **ANTIBIOTICS** help to finally destroy all the germs.

8. **NORMAL** health is restored.

AIDS-INFECTED IMMUNE SYSTEM (SE-46)

DIRECTIONS: Fill in the blanks using the words below to explain what happens to the AIDS infected immune system.

KAPOSI'S	B-CELLS	"FACTORIES"	ATTACHES
T-CELLS	HIV	CANNOT	ANTIBODIES
DESTROYED	DIE	PNEUMONIA	OPPORTUNISTIC
DEMENTIA			

© 1993 by The Center for Applied Research in Education

1. The _____**HIV**_____ invades the body and quickly multiplies.

2. The immune system tries to fight back by sending white blood cells to destroy the invaders.

3. _____**T-CELLS**_____ surround and attempt to "eat" the HIV

4. but the HIV _____**ATTACHES**_____ itself to the T-cells causing

them to become HIV-producing _____**"FACTORIES"**_____.

5. The T-cells _____**CANNOT**_____ chemically notify

the _____**B-CELLS**_____ , and therefore,

6. the _____**B-CELLS**_____ cannot produce _____**ANTIBODIES**_____.

7. The immune system is _____**DESTROYED**_____ and the person is susceptible to

many _____**OPPORTUNISTIC**_____ diseases, such as:

8. Pneumocystis carinii _____**PNEUMONIA**_____ , _____**KAPOSI'S**_____

sarcoma, and AIDS _____**DEMENTIA**_____ complex.

9. These diseases usually cause the person to _____**DIE**_____ .

137

HOW AIDS IS SPREAD (SE-47)

1. SEX: <u>ORAL</u>

   <u>ANAL</u>

   <u>VAGINAL</u>

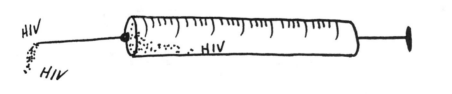

2. **Blood transfusion with** <u>CONTAMINATED</u> **blood or blood products.**

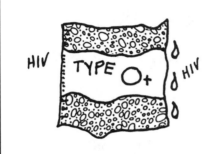

3. **Using contaminated IV drug** <u>NEEDLES</u> .

4. **From** <u>MOTHER</u> **to baby at birth.**

HOW AIDS IS NOT SPREAD (SE-48)

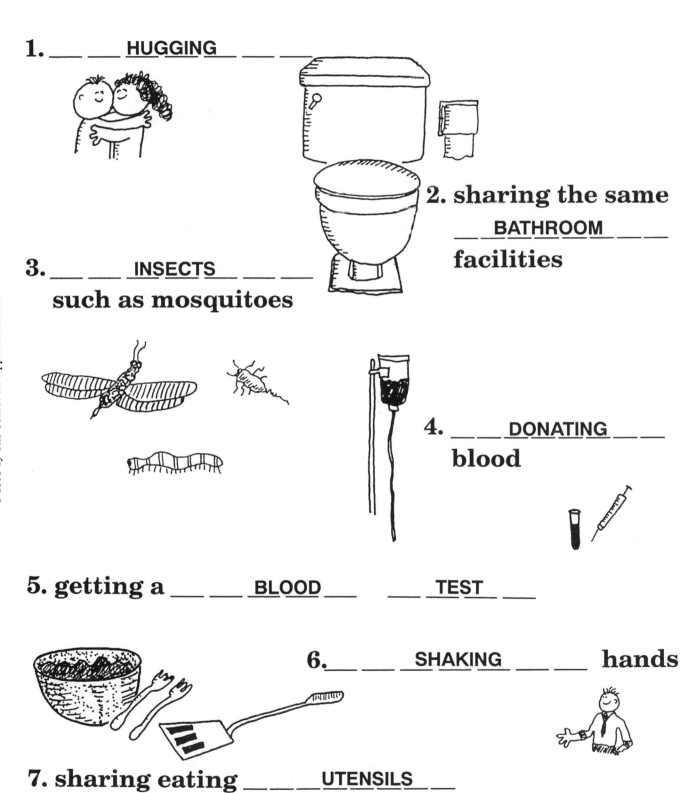

1. ___ ___ HUGGING ___ ___ ___

2. **sharing the same** ___ BATHROOM ___ ___ **facilities**

3. ___ ___ INSECTS ___ ___ ___ **such as mosquitoes**

4. ___ ___ DONATING ___ ___ **blood**

5. **getting a** ___ ___ BLOOD ___ ___ TEST ___

6. ___ ___ SHAKING ___ ___ **hands**

7. **sharing eating** ___ ___ ___ UTENSILS ___ ___

HOW THE AIDS VIRUS CAN AFFECT YOU (SE-49)

DIRECTIONS: Using the words in the answer box, write the best answer in the blank.

HOW THE AIDS VIRUS CAN AFFECT YOU:

1. *Asymptomatic*

You could have the HIV in your body and have no _____**SIGNS**_____ or _____**SYMPTOMS**_____. You could appear _____**HEALTHY**_____ but still pass the disease to others.

2. *ARC (AIDS Related Complex)*

A person infected with the HIV could have some _____**EARLY**_____ symptoms of AIDS, such as fatigue, diarrhea, _____**FEVER**_____, swollen lymph nodes, loss of _____**APPETITE**_____, weight loss, skin _____**RASHES**_____, and night _____**SWEATS**_____.

3. *AIDS*

This is developed 6 months to 10 years after infection. Once you have AIDS you will live from 6 months to 3 years. AIDS patients usually die of an _____**OPPORTUNISTIC**_____ _____**DISEASE**_____, such as pneumocystis carinii pneumonia, Kaposi's sarcoma, or AIDS dementia complex. People with healthy immune systems do not get these diseases.

TO AVOID AIDS:

1. Practice abstinence—no _____**SEX**_____.
2. Practice monogamy—one _____**PARTNER**_____.
3. Use a _____**CONDOM**_____ treated with nonoxynol-9.
4. Don't use illegal IV drugs and don't share _____**NEEDLES**_____.
5. Don't share objects that get _____**BLOOD**_____ on them, such as razors or toothbrushes.

BLOOD	NEEDLES	CONDOM	EARLY	SEX
HEALTHY	PARTNER	RASHES	APPETITE	FEVER
SWEATS	SYMPTOMS	SIGNS	OPPORTUNISTIC	DISEASE

AIDS TRUE/FALSE WORKSHEET (SE-50)

DIRECTIONS: On the line to the left, write T if the statement is true. If the statement is not true, replace the underlined words with words that would make the statement true.

T-CELLS   1. The HIV is most likely to attack the <u>B cells</u>.

T   2. <u>Antibodies</u> are proteins that destroy foreign substances.

ELISA   3. The first test given to determine the presence of AIDS antibodies is the <u>Western Blot</u> test.

VIRUS   4. AIDS is caused by a <u>fungus</u>.

T   5. Being protected from disease means you are <u>immune</u>.

MONOGAMY   6. Having one sexual partner is called <u>bigamy</u>.

BISEXUAL   7. A <u>heterosexual</u> has sexual partners of both sexes.

SEMEN   8. HIV is found in the highest concentrations in blood, vaginal secretions, and <u>urine</u>.

ABSTINENCE   9. The best way to avoid getting AIDS is <u>using a condom</u>.

IMMUNE   10. AIDS destroys the body's <u>digestive</u> system, leaving the victim susceptible to other diseases.